The Annotated Ring Cycle

An English Reading Version of
The Nibelung's Ring
by Richard Wagner

Twilight for the Gods (Götterdämmerung)

Translation and Annotations
by Frederick Paul Walter

AMADEUS PRESS
Lanham • Boulder • New York • London

Published by Amadeus Press
An imprint of The Rowman & Littlefield Publishing Group, Inc.
4501 Forbes Boulevard, Suite 200, Lanham, Maryland 20706
www.rowman.com

86-90 Paul Street, London EC2A 4NE, United Kingdom

Copyright © 2022 by The Rowman & Littlefield Publishing Group, Inc.

All rights reserved. No part of this book may be reproduced in any form or by any electronic or mechanical means, including information storage and retrieval systems, without written permission from the publisher, except by a reviewer who may quote passages in a review.

British Library Cataloguing in Publication Information Available

Library of Congress Cataloging-in-Publication Data

Names: Wagner, Richard, 1813–1883, author. | Walter, Frederick Paul, translator. | Wagner, Richard, 1813–1883. Ring des Nibelungen. Götterdämmerung (Libretto). English.
Title: The annotated ring cycle : Twilight for the Gods (Götterdämmerung) / translation and annotations by Frederick Paul Walter.
Other titles: Ring des Nibelungen. Götterdämmerung (Libretto)
Description: Lanham : Amadeus, 2022. | Includes bibliographical references. | German, with English translation; annotations in English.
Identifiers: LCCN 2021056823 (print) | LCCN 2021056824 (ebook) | ISBN 9781538136669 (paperback) | ISBN 9781538136676 (epub)
Subjects: LCSH: Wagner, Richard, 1813–1883. Ring des Nibelungen. | Operas—Librettos. | LCGFT: Librettos.
Classification: LCC ML50.W14 R72 2022 (print) | LCC ML50.W14 (ebook) | DDC 782.1/0268—dc23
LC record available at https://lccn.loc.gov/2021056823
LC ebook record available at https://lccn.loc.gov/2021056824

Contents

The 1-Minute Ring — v

Chronology: The Composition of the Ring Cycle — vii

Introduction — ix

Timeline of the Ring Cycle to Date — xi

Prologue and Act 1 — 1

Act 2 — 69

Act 3 — 121

Timeline of the Entire Ring Cycle — 167

What the Cycle Does . . . and Doesn't — 171

Related Resources — 175

About the Contributors — 179

THE 1-MINUTE RING

A. Dwarf steals gold from river; god recovers gold but gives it to giants. (*The Rhine Gold*)
B. God schemes to recover gold from giant and return it to river; fails. (*The Valkyrie*)
C. Dwarves scheme to recover gold from giant and keep it; human keeps it instead. (*Siegfried*)
D. Dwarves scheme to recover gold from humans; fail. Human returns it to river. (*Twilight for the Gods*)

- Time frame: 3 generations.
- Motives: wealth, fame, power, justice, fear of death, humane love, and sexual love.
- Consequences: 1 attempted murder, 2 manslaughters, 3 capital murders, 4 adulteries, many combat mortalities, multiple betrayals, countless deceptions, mass enslavement, self-immolation, and full regime change.

CHRONOLOGY: THE COMPOSITION OF THE RING CYCLE

1848   October–November: Wagner pens *The Nibelung Myth as a Scenario for a Play*, plus prose and verse drafts of *Siegfried's Death* (later called *Twilight for the Gods*.)

1851   May–November: Wagner pens prose and verse drafts of *Siegfried*, plus treatments of the two remaining operas.

1852   March–November: Wagner pens prose and verse drafts of *The Rhine Gold* and *The Valkyrie*.

1853   February: Wagner privately publishes the libretto for his entire *The Nibelung's Ring*.

1854   January–September: Wagner composes the full score of *The Rhine Gold* and begins *The Valkyrie*.

1855–56   Wagner completes the full score of *The Valkyrie* and begins *Siegfried*.

1857   January–August: Wagner completes the full score of *Siegfried* Act 1 and the piano score of Act 2.

1864–65   Wagner completes the full score of *Siegfried* Act 2.

1869   March: Wagner begins composing *Siegfried* Act 3.
September: Munich offers a stand-alone staging of *The Rhine Gold* at King Ludwig II's behest.
October: Wagner begins composing *Twilight for the Gods*.

1870   June: Munich offers a stand-alone staging of *The Valkyrie* at King Ludwig II's behest.

1871   February: Wagner completes the full score of *Siegfried*.

1874   November: Wagner completes the full score of *Twilight for the Gods*.

1876   August: Bayreuth premieres *The Nibelung's Ring*, offering three complete performances rehearsed by Wagner himself.

Introduction

This is the final volume of *The Annotated Ring Cycle*. The first three installments, *The Rhine Gold*, *The Valkyrie*, and *Siegfried*, have now brought us to the climax of Wagner's operatic colossus *The Nibelung's Ring*. We've witnessed the theft of gold from the Rhine River by a vindictive dwarf, Alberich the Nibelung; his forging of the gold into a tyrannical Ring of Power; then the ring's repeatedly changing hands due to the abortive efforts of Wotan, leader of the gods, to thwart the dwarf's schemes of world domination. Wotan captures the ring, gives it to the giant Fafner to pay off a debt, breeds a tribe of heroes to retrieve it, fails wretchedly, and finally abdicates, leaving his daughter Brünnhilde and grandson Siegfried to restore peace to the planet.

As this outline indicates, Wagner's four-part theater piece is the ancestor of three pop-culture phenomena: J. R. R. Tolkien's trilogy *The Lord of the Rings*, George Lucas's *Star Wars* franchise, and J. K. Rowling's septet of Harry Potter novels. The fraternal twins Luke and Leia echo the persecuted siblings Siegmund and Sieglinde in *The Valkyrie*; Alberich, the Cycle's power-mad dwarf, is the forerunner of both Gollum and Voldemort; and the three wise men of these sagas—Gandalf, Obi-Wan Kenobi, and Dumbledore—are all versions of Wagner's wily old Wanderer, actually the god Wotan in his enlightened senior years.

So this will seem familiar territory even to folks visiting it for the first time. Consequently, *The Annotated Ring Cycle* is targeted not only to operagoers but also readers and devotees of fantasy fiction. These volumes focus on the Cycle's *storyline*: its libretto, lyrics, and stage business; its motives, personalities, and plot twists; what literally happens onstage; what its *narrative* shows and tells us about itself.

My intent for this new translation is to provide a reading version in clear, modern English that hints at Wagner's style, from his alliterative effects to his humor, colloquialisms, and occasional rhyme schemes. My notes center on what's clearly onstage, staying with what the text itself reveals. In addition, I follow the work's major subdivisions with retrospective, one-page recaps as memory tools—but feel free to skip them if you wish.

Regarding Wagner's musical fabric, I normally confine my remarks to moments where it supplies information or ambiance not conveyed by the lyrics or stage directions. For readers who want more detail on Wagner's system of motifs, I recommend Deryck Cooke's long-admired *An Introduction to* Der Ring des Nibelungen.

As for this climactic volume, it closes with an extended backward glance: it explores both what the Cycle accomplishes and the questions it leaves unanswered. The final section, "Related Resources," is an annotated bibliography—my personal selection from the myriad Wagner commentaries that I consider the most stimulating, perceptive, or both.

As before, I hope newcomers and old-timers will each find that these volumes add pleasure and value to their experience of the most colossal achievement in the performing arts, Richard Wagner's *The Nibelung's Ring*.

1911 PEN DRAWING BY ARTHUR RACKHAM

TIMELINE OF THE RING CYCLE TO DATE

Preamble: *The Rhine Gold*

* Alberich meets the Rhine daughters and steals their gold.
    — He forges it into a magic ring.
    — He enslaves his fellow Nibelungs.

* Wotan, a good ruler going bad, hires Fasolt and Fafner to build him a royal castle.
    — They ask to be paid with Alberich's stolen gold.
    — Instead of returning the gold to the Rhine, Wotan agrees to this.
    — He and Loge capture Alberich in his underground realm.
    — They take Alberich's treasure, tarnhelmet, and ring.
    — Alberich puts a curse on the ring, promising misery and doom to wearers.

* Wotan hands the treasure to the giants but holds on to the ring.
    — The oracle Erda urges him to give it up.
    — He turns it over to the giants and fulfills his agreement.

* Fafner kills Fasolt and hides in a forest.
    — He changes into a dragon to guard the ring and treasure.

* The gods dwell in their new castle, now called Valhalla.
    — Wotan sees the ring is a danger and must be returned to the Rhine.
    — Going from bad to worse, he devises a scheme for getting around his agreement.

TIMELINE OF THE RING CYCLE TO DATE

Day 1: *The Valkyrie* . . .

* Wotan mates with a human woman.
    — She bears him fraternal twins, Siegmund and Sieglinde.
    — Wotan trains Siegmund and gives him a magic sword for killing Fafner.
    — The twins become lovers.

* Loge leaves the gods and changes back into a fire spirit.

* Wotan visits the oracle Erda to gain knowledge.
    — She bears him nine daughters, Brünnhilde and the Valkyries.
    — They raise an army of slain warriors to guard Valhalla from Alberich.

* Fricka shows Wotan that his plan would destroy both his regime and his legacy.
    — Siegmund's seizure of the ring would demolish them as promptly as if Wotan seized it himself.
    — It would topple the two ethical pillars the god has erected, fair dealing and truth telling.
    — They, at least, can remain after him (and do), but not if he himself has undermined them.

* Wotan orders Siegmund's death, but Brünnhilde tries to save the twins.
    — The god intervenes and breaks Siegmund's sword; Siegmund dies.
    — Pregnant with Siegmund's son, Sieglinde flees with the broken sword.
    — Wotan punishes Brünnhilde, leaving her asleep behind a wall of fire.
    — He grounds the Valkyries and their zombie army.
    — Reaching his rock bottom, Wotan recognizes his powerlessness.

Day 2: *Siegfried*

* Wotan goes on a pilgrimage for nearly a generation.
    — Dressed as a wanderer, he seeks further wisdom.

* Meanwhile, the pregnant Sieglinde collapses in a forest close to the dragon's lair.
    — She's rescued by the dwarf Mime and dies giving birth to Siegfried.
    — Mime raises the boy to slay the dragon and capture the ring.

* Wotan returns but avoids Siegfried, so the boy remains independent.
    — Instead, he offers aid to Mime and Alberich, with no immediate result.

* Siegfried reforges the broken sword.
    — Mime manipulates him into slaying Fafner.
    — The boy takes the ring and tarnhelmet without breaking Wotan's agreement.
    — Mime tries to kill him but dies when Siegfried strikes first.
    — A Woodbird guides Siegfried to a girl who can be his companion.

* Wotan blocks the boy's way, deliberately provoking a showdown.
    — Siegfried smashes his scepter and ends the god's rule.

* Siegfried finds the sleeping Brünnhilde, wakes her, and weds her.

Richard Wagner
TWILIGHT FOR THE GODS
(GÖTTERDÄMMERUNG)

Day 3 of the festival drama
The Nibelung's Ring

Humans
- Siegfried, *tenor* — orphan son of Siegmund and Sieglinde
- Brünnhilde, *soprano* — former Valkyrie, the twins' half sister
- Gunther, *baritone* — head of the Gibichung clan
- Gutrune, *soprano* — his sister
- Hagen, *bass* — their half brother
- Gibichung clanspeople, *chorus* — soldiers, servants, ladies-in-waiting

Gods
- Waltraute — Valkyrie and Brünnhilde's sister
- 1st Norn, *contralto* — daughter of the oracle Erda
- 2nd Norn, *mezzo-soprano* — her sister
- 3rd Norn, *soprano* — also her sister

Nibelungs
- Alberich, *baritone* — dwarf

Rhine daughters
- Woglinde, *soprano* — water sprite
- Wellgunde, *soprano* — water sprite; her sister
- Flosshilde, *mezzo-soprano* — water sprite; also her sister

Time: the age of northern myth . . . same generation as Day 2.

ACT 1

ACT 1

Prelude and Prologue

The curtain slowly opens on the Valkyrie's mountain, the same setting as at the close of Day 2. It's night. Far upstage, flames are glowing. We see the three Norns, tall female forms draped in dark robes like long veils. The 1st Norn (the eldest) is lying downstage audience left under a fir tree with wide branches; the 2nd Norn (younger in years) is stretched out on a stony ridge in front of the cave opening; the 3rd Norn (the youngest) is seated upstage center by a jutting rock. All is somber, silent, and still.

1ST NORN

Welch Licht leuchtet dort? — What's that glowing light?

2ND NORN

Dämmert der Tag schon auf? — Is the dawn glimmering already?

3RD NORN

Loges Heer — Loge's forces are
lodert feurig um den Fels. — protecting the peak with lurid flames.
Noch ist's Nacht. — The night isn't over.
Was spinnen und singen wir nicht? — Shouldn't we spin and sing?

2ND NORN
(To the 1st Norn)

Wollen wir spinnen und singen, — If the three of us sing and spin,
woran spannst du das Seil? — where will you secure the thread?

1ST NORN
(Unwinding the golden thread from around her, [1] she ties one end to a branch of the fir tree.)

So gut und schlimm es geh', — However it turns out, I'll take up
schling ich das Seil und singe. — the thread and spin my tale.
An der Weltesche — By the World Ash Tree [2]
wob ich einst, — I used to weave,
da groß und stark — when its trunk
dem Stamm entgrünte — was tall, firm, and green,
weihlicher Äste Wald. — a forest of blessed branches.
Im kühlen Schatten — In the cool of its shade
rauscht ein Quell, — a spring came to be,
Weisheit raunend — a well of wisdom
rann sein Gewell': — beneath the tree—
da sang ich heil'gen Sinn. — there I sang my sacred thoughts.
Ein kühner Gott — A daring god
trat zum Trunk an den Quell; — sought to drink from the spring; [3]
seiner Augen eines — he gave one of his eyes
zahlt' er als ewigen Zoll. — to pay for this privilege.
Von der Weltesche — From the World Ash Tree
brach da Wotan einen Ast; — Wotan broke off a branch;

ACT 1

[1] Another gold article in addition to Alberich's ring, Freia's apples, and Fricka's whip—is the thread of destiny also a symbol of domination?

[2] As our notes mentioned in *The Rhine Gold*, "some of its events have backstories that are narrated later." The Norns will now share those backstories, plus some current developments.

[3] Wotan seems to have had honorable motives in seeking out this "well of wisdom"—the insights he gained from the experience evidently included his ideals of fair dealing and truth telling.

ACT 1

eines Speeres Schaft	he whittled the shaft
entschnitt der Starke dem Stamm.	of his spear from its wood. [1]
In langer Zeiten Lauf	As time went by,
zehrte die Wunde den Wald;	the wound in the tree grew worse;
falb fielen die Blätter,	its leaves dropped off,
dürr darbte der Baum;	and its trunk decayed;
traurig versiegte	to my sorrow
des Quelles Trank;	the spring ran dry; [2]
trüben Sinnes	mournful thoughts
ward mein Gesang.	marred my singing.
Doch web' ich heut	Today I don't weave
an der Weltesche nicht mehr,	by the World Ash Tree
muß mir die Tanne	but must use this fir
taugen, zu fesseln das Seil:	for fastening the thread—
singe, Schwester,	sing, sister,
dir werf ich's zu.	I throw it to you.
Weißt du wie das wird?	Can you say what will come?

2ND NORN
(She catches the thread, then winds it around a point of rock by the cave opening.)

Treu berat'ner	Ethical agreements
Verträge Runen	were recorded in the runes
schnitt Wotan	Wotan etched
in des Speeres Schaft:	on the shaft of his spear—
den hielt er als Haft der Welt.	his scepter for ruling the earth. [3]
Ein kühner Held	A courageous hero
zerhieb im Kampfe den Speer;	smashed the spear in a confrontation;
in Trümmer sprang	he sliced in half
der Verträge heiliger Haft.	this holy archive of agreements.
Da hieß Wotan	Then Wotan had
Walhalls Helden,	Valhalla's heroes
der Weltesche	visit the World Ash Tree
welkes Geäst	to hew it down
mit dem Stamm in Stücke zu fällen:	and hack up its withered branches—
die Esche sank;	the Ash Tree fell;
ewig versiegte der Quell.	its spring stayed dry for good.
Feßle ich heut	Today I fasten
an dem scharfen Fels das Seil:	the thread to a sharp rock—
singe, Schwester,	sing, sister,
dir werf ich's zu.	I throw it to you.
Weißt du wie das wird?	Can you say what will come?

3RD NORN
(Catching the end of the thread and winding it behind herself)

Es ragt die Burg,	The castle endures
von Riesen gebaut:	that the giants erected—
mit der Götter und Helden	with his goodly retinue
heiliger Sippe	of gods and warriors

ACT 1

[1] And with this action he undertook his calling: protector of oaths and agreements.

[2] Mirroring Wotan's deterioration into vanity, obsession with permanence, and fear of death.

[3] A fruit of the wisdom he acquired from the spring. Taking on the role of guardian of justice (*der die Rechte währt*), Wotan made a well-intentioned effort to bring order into the world, defending oaths (to promote truth telling) and agreements (to promote fair dealing). Unfortunately, good intentions are rarely enough.

ACT 1

sitzt dort Wotan im Saal.	Wotan waits in its throne room.
Gehau'ner Scheite	Hewed into pieces,
hohe Schicht	huge logs
ragt zu Hauf	lie in piles
rings um die Halle:	around the palace—
die Weltesche war dies einst!	all that's left of the World Ash Tree!
Brennt das Holz	When this wood blazes
heilig brünstig und hell,	into a blessed holocaust
sengt die Glut	and its flames
sehrend den glänzenden Saal,	devour that glittering fortress,
der ewigen Götter Ende	twilight will descend on the gods,
dämmert ewig da auf.	and they'll pass away for good.
Wisset ihr noch?	Like to learn more?
So windet von neuem das Seil;	Then rewind the thread;
von Norden wieder	I throw it from the north
werf ich's dir nach.	to hear something new.

(She tosses the thread to the 2nd Norn; the latter hands it off to the 1st Norn, who unfastens it from the branch and ties it to a different one.)

Spinne, Schwester, und singe!	Spin, sister, and sing to us!

1ST NORN
(Looking upstage as she proceeds)

Dämmert der Tag?	Is that the dawning daylight?
Oder leuchtet die Lohe?	Or the flickering of the fire?
Getrübt trügt sich mein Blick;	My troubled eyes are playing tricks;
nicht hell eracht ich	I can't discern
das heilig Alte,	the distant past
da Loge einst	when Loge first
brannte in lichter Glut.	broke into brilliant flames.
Weißt du was aus ihm ward?	Can you say what came of him?

2ND NORN
(Again winding the thread around the rock)

Durch des Speeres Zauber	With the magic in his spear
zähmte ihn Wotan;	Wotan subdued him;
Räte raunt' er dem Gott:	he gave the god advice—
an des Schaftes Runen,	which ate into the runes
frei sich zu raten,	on its shaft,
nagte zehrend sein Zahn.	then he attempted to run away.
Da mit des Speeres	So, with the power
zwingender Spitze	of his spearpoint,
bannte ihn Wotan,	Wotan made him
Brünnhildes Fels zu umbrennen.	burn around Brünnhilde's mountain.

(She throws the thread to the 3rd Norn, who again winds it behind herself.)

Weißt du was aus ihm wird?	Can you say what will come of him?

ACT 1

"Take up the thread, sisters!"
1914 ILLUSTRATION BY FRANZ STASSEN

ACT 1

3RD NORN

Des zerschlag'nen Speeres	The two pieces
stechende Splitter	of the shattered spear
taucht einst Wotan	Wotan will plunge
dem Brünstigen tief in die Brust:	into Loge's fiery breast—
zehrender Brand	they'll burst into
zündet da auf;	furious flame;
den wirft der Gott	then the god will hurl them
in der Weltesche	onto the Ash Tree's logs
zu Hauf geschichtete Scheite.	that lie heaped all around. [1]

(She throws the thread back; the 2nd Norn gathers it and throws it to the 1st Norn again.)

Wollt ihr wissen	Can you tell us
wann das wird?	when this will come?
Schwinget, Schwestern, das Seil!	Take up the thread, sisters!

1ST NORN
(Tying the thread again.)

Die Nacht weicht;	The night's going away;
nichts mehr gewahr ich:	nothing's clear any longer—
des Seiles Fäden	these lengths of thread
find ich nicht mehr;	are giving me trouble;
verflochten ist das Geflecht.	they've gotten twisted and tangled.
Ein wüstes Gesicht	Cloudy prospects
wirrt mir wütend den Sinn:	throw my thoughts into confusion—
das Rheingold	Alberich once robbed
raubte Alberich einst:	the gold from the Rhine— [2]
weißt du was aus ihm ward?	can you say what came of him?

2ND NORN
(Struggling to loop the thread around the sharp-edged rock by the cave opening)

Des Steines Schärfe	The sharpness of the stone
schnitt in das Seil;	threatens to tear the thread;
nicht fest spannt mehr	its lengths daren't stretch
der Fäden Gespinst;	tightly any longer;
verwirrt ist das Geweb'.	the pattern's loosening.
aus Not und Neid	It's from the havoc and hatred
ragt mir des Niblungen Ring:	caused by the Nibelung's ring—
ein rächender Fluch	his vengeful curse
nagt meiner Fäden Geflecht.	eats into the vanishing pattern.

(Throwing the thread to the 3rd Norn) [3]

Weißt du was daraus wird?	Can you say what will come next?

3RD NORN
(Hurriedly snatching at it)

Zu locker das Seil,	The thread's too slack,
mir langt es nicht.	it's not stretching to me.

ACT 1

[1] An essential detail that audiences sometimes miss: Wotan himself will torch Valhalla and bring about the gods' passing.

[2] Like the Rhine daughters and the Cycle's own stage directions, the Norns also call Alberich a thief. Yet Alberich doesn't admit this himself, as we've seen.

[3] Meanwhile two partial motifs suddenly spurt from the orchestra, the beginning of Alberich's curse on the ring, then a snatch of Siegfried's horn call. What have they to do with each other?

ACT 1

Soll ich nach Norden	To tug this end
neigen das Ende,	toward the north,
straffer sei es gestreckt!	I need it to be tauter!

(She pulls on the thread; it snaps.)

Es riß!	It snapped! [1]

2ND NORN

Es riß!	It snapped!

1ST NORN

Es riß!	It snapped!

(The Norns retreat in horror to center stage; they gather the broken lengths of thread and tie themselves together.)

THE THREE NORNS

Zu End' ewiges Wissen!	Pass away, perpetual wisdom!
Der Welt melden	The world no longer
Weise nichts mehr.	will learn from us.

3RD NORN

Hinab!	Into the earth!

2ND NORN

Zur Mutter!	Back to mother!

1ST NORN

Hinab!	Into the earth!

(They vanish from view. [2] As the rosy dawn grows brighter, the firelight below grows fainter. The sun comes up. It's broad daylight. Siegfried and Brünnhilde emerge from the cave opening. He's in full armor, she's leading her horse by the bridle.)

BRÜNNHILDE

Zu neuen Taten,	You long for adventure,
teurer Helde,	my sweet hero,
wie liebt' ich dich,	so how could I love you
ließ ich dich nicht?	and not let you seek it? [3]
Ein einzig' Sorgen	A tiny doubt
läßt mich säumen,	troubles me,
daß dir zu wenig	that you haven't received
mein Wert gewann.	the rewards you deserve.
Was Götter mich wiesen,	What the gods taught me
gab ich dir:	I've given you—
heiliger Runen	a rich supply
reichen Hort;	of runic wisdom;

ACT 1

[1] And now the brass sound Alberich's full curse:

Did that allusion to Siegfried's horn call mean he's the next victim? In any case the thread of destiny is broken. Nobody knows what lies ahead.

[2] And depart forever without offering any new information or insights on Alberich.

[3] Siegfried's been eager to see the world since the day we met him.

ACT 1

doch meiner Stärke	but the powers of
magdlichen Stamm	my prized virginity
nahm mir der Held,	were taken from me
dem ich nun mich neige.	by the hero who tamed me.
Des Wissens bar,	So I've no further learning
doch des Wunsches voll;	but am full of desire,
an Liebe reich,	I've a storehouse of love
doch ledig der Kraft:	but no other strengths—
mögst du die Arme	please don't condemn
nicht verachten,	this poor creature
die dir nur gönnen,	who'd grudge you nothing
nicht geben mehr kann!	but has nothing more to give!

SIEGFRIED

Mehr gabst du Wunderfrau,	You wondrous woman, you gave more
als ich zu wahren weiß.	than my wits can master.
Nicht zürne, wenn dein Lehren	Don't be dismayed when your lessons
mich unbelehret ließ!	are difficult for me to learn!
Ein Wissen doch wahr ich wohl:	One topic you've truly taught me—

(Passionately)

daß mir Brünnhilde lebt;	that I have Brünnhilde's love;
eine Lehre lernt ich leicht:	one subject was simple to learn—
Brünnhildes zu gedenken!	to keep Brünnhilde always in mind!

BRÜNNHILDE

Willst du mir Minne schenken,	Don't ever leave our love behind,
gedenke deiner nur,	but remember yourself,
gedenke deiner Taten:	remember your feats—
gedenk des wilden Feuers,	remember the blazing fire
das furchtlos du durchschrittest,	barricading this peak
da den Fels es rings umbrann!	that you fearlessly penetrated!

SIEGFRIED

Brünnhilde zu gewinnen!	To win Brünnhilde!

BRÜNNHILDE

Gedenk der beschildeten Frau,	Remember the woman wearing armor,
die in tiefem Schlaf du fandest,	whom you found fast asleep,
der den festen Helm du erbrachst!	whose tight-fitting helmet you took off!

SIEGFRIED

Brünnhilde zu erwecken!	To wake Brünnhilde!

BRÜNNHILDE

Gedenk der Eide,	Remember the oaths
die uns einen;	that make us one;

ACT 1

1876 costume design for Brünnhilde during Day 3 by Carl Emil Doepler.

ACT 1

gedenk der Treue,	remember the fidelity
die wir tragen;	we've pledged forever;
gedenk der Liebe,	remember the love
der wir leben:	we live for—
Brünnhilde brennt dann ewig	then Brünnhilde will eternally burn
heilig dir in der Brust!	as a holy flame in your heart!

(She hugs Siegfried.)

SIEGFRIED

Laß ich, Liebste, dich hier	I'm leaving you here, my love,
in der Lohe heiliger Hut,	in the fire's holy protection,

(Slipping Alberich's ring from his finger and giving it to Brünnhilde)

zum Tausche deiner Runen	and in exchange for your runic wisdom,
reich ich dir diesen Ring.	receive this ring from me.
Was der Taten je ich schuf,	It enshrines my adventures
des Tugend schließt er ein.	and accomplishments.
Ich erschlug einen wilden Wurm,	I slew a savage dragon
der grimmig lang ihn bewacht.	that grimly guarded it for decades.
nun wahre du seine Kraft	I leave it in your safekeeping
als Weihegruß meiner Treu!	as a symbol of my loyalty! [1]

BRÜNNHILDE
(Delightedly slipping it on)

Ihn geiz ich als einziges Gut!	It's my most precious possession!
Für den Ring nimm nun auch mein Roß!	And in place of the ring, receive my horse!
Ging sein Lauf mit mir	In the past he carried me
einst kühn durch die Lüfte,	courageously through the air,
mit mir	but like myself,
verlor es die mächt'ge Art;	he lost his magic powers;
über Wolken hin	through storm clouds
auf blitzenden Wettern	and lightning bolts
nicht mehr	he never again
schwingt es sich mutig des Wegs;	will boldly streak on his way;
doch wohin du ihn führst,	but on the ground you can guide him
sei es durchs Feuer,	even through fire,
grauenlos folgt dir Grane:	and Grane will fearlessly follow—
denn dir, o Helde,	because, my hero,
soll es gehorchen.	he'll always heed you.
Du hüt ihn wohl;	Take good care of him;
er hört dein Wort:	he'll obey your commands.
O, bringe Grane	And often bring Grane
oft Brünnhildes Gruß!	greetings from Brünnhilde!

SIEGFRIED

Durch deine Tugend allein	So you're my sole inspiration
soll so ich Taten noch wirken?	when I seek out adventure?

ACT 1

[1] Siegfried has acquired an air of courtliness and dignity since his lusty first encounter with Brünnhilde. No doubt her influence is responsible for his chivalric manners—as a Valkyrie she interacted professionally with the warriors and lords of the day.

ACT 1

Meine Kämpfe kiesest du,	Then choose my challenges,
meine Siege kehren zu dir:	take credit for my conquests—
auf deines Rosses Rücken,	when I straddle your steed,
in deines Schildes Schirm,	in the shelter of your shield,
nicht Siegfried acht ich mich mehr,	I'm not Siegfried anymore,
ich bin nur Brünnhildes Arm.	I'm simply Brünnhilde's sword arm!

BRÜNNHILDE

O wäre Brünnhild' deine Seele!	Then Brünnhilde is with you in spirit!

SIEGFRIED

Durch sie entbrennt mir der Mut.	She sparks the courage in my breast.

BRÜNNHILDE

So wärst du Siegfried und Brünnhild'?	So you're both Siegfried *and* Brünnhilde?

SIEGFRIED
(Tenderly)

Wo ich bin, bergen sich beide.	Wherever I wander, she's there as well.

BRÜNNHILDE
(Excitedly)

So verödet mein Felsensaal?	So this summit isn't occupied?

SIEGFRIED

Vereint faßt er uns zwei!	Since we're one, we stay here too!

BRÜNNHILDE
(In an outburst of emotion)

Oh! heilige Götter!	Oh, you gods in the sky!
Hehre Geschlechter!	My sacred family!
Weidet eu'r Aug'	Feast your eyes
an dem weihvollen Paar!	on this fortunate couple!
Getrennt—wer will es scheiden?	Apart—who could separate us?
Geschieden—trennt es sich nie!	Together—we'll never part!

SIEGFRIED

Heil dir, Brünnhilde,	Hail, Brünnhilde,
prangender Stern!	brilliant star!
Heil, strahlende Liebe!	Hail to our splendid love!

BRÜNNHILDE

Heil dir, Siegfried,	Hail, Siegfried,
siegendes Licht!	beacon of success!
Heil, strahlendes Leben!	Hail to our splendid life!

ACT 1

Brünnhilde watches Siegfried descend.
1911 WATERCOLOR BY ARTHUR RACKHAM

ACT 1

	BOTH	
Heil! Heil! Heil! Heil!		Hail! Hail! Hail! Hail!

(Siegfried leads his horse briskly along the cliff edge while Brünnhilde follows. Hero and horse vanish behind an outcrop and are no longer visible to the audience; now left alone by the cliff edge, Brünnhilde watches Siegfried descend. Her movements indicate that he's gone out of sight. Siegfried's horn is audible from below. Brünnhilde cocks an ear. She moves closer to the edge. Now she spots Siegfried again in the distance—she waves merrily to him. Her cheery smile shows that the carefree hero is still in sight. The curtain closes quickly.)

1910 PEN DRAWING BY ARTHUR RACKHAM

ACT 1
LOOKING BACK ON THE PROLOGUE

News hour with the Norns—
1) Old news:
    - ... Young Wotan visited the World Ash Tree and paid one of his eyes to drink from its "well of wisdom."
    - ... Next he broke off a branch from the Ash Tree and carved it into a spear.
    - ... With this scepter he ruled as defender of agreements and oaths.
    - ... The Ash Tree's deterioration mirrored his own deterioration.
    - ... His rule ended when Siegfried snapped his spear in two.
2) Breaking news:
    - ... Wotan had the World Ash Tree chopped down and piled around Valhalla.
    - ... With his warrior guard and the other gods, Wotan waits in his throne room for the end.
    - ... When it's time, he'll ignite the chopped logs, burn down Valhalla, and bring about the gods' passing.
3) Updates on Alberich:
    - ... None.

Concerning the happy couple—
1) They're adoring spouses in a common-law marriage and have sworn lifelong fidelity.
2) Brunnhilde has given Siegfried runic wisdom and training in chivalric traditions.
3) They're sincerely in love, but Siegfried still longs to see the outside world.
4) Brünnhilde agrees, and they exchange going-away presents.
5) They promise to remain with each other in spirit.

As for the ring—
It's changed hands again.

ACT 1

Scene 1

The Gibichung villa on the Rhine River

(The curtain opens. [1] The villa's walls gape at the rear and reveal the riverbank; rugged cliffs frame the shoreline. Gunther and Gutrune are seated on thrones to the side, behind a table with liquid refreshments; Hagen sits downstage of it.)

GUNTHER

Nun hör, Hagen;	Hear me out, Hagen, [2]
sage mir, Held:	advise me, good hero—
sitz ich herrlich am Rhein,	what is Gunther's stature on the Rhine,
Gunther zu Gibichs Ruhm?	am I spreading the Gibichungs' fame?

HAGEN

Dich echt genannten	You're the legitimate brother
acht ich zu neiden;	and your life is enviable;
die beid' uns Brüder gebar,	she who bore us both,
Frau Grimhild' ließ mich's begreifen.	Lady Grimhilde, bred me to look up to you.

GUNTHER

Dich neide ich;	I'm envious of you,
nicht neide mich du.	you've no reason for envy.
Erbt' ich Erstlingsart,	I'm the royal heir,
Weisheit ward dir allein:	but you inherited the wisdom—
Halbbrüder Zwist	we're half brothers
bezwang sich nie besser.	who work well together.
Deinem Rat nur red ich Lob,	I'm complimenting your counsel
frag ich dich nach meinem Ruhm.	when I ask you about my fame. [3]

HAGEN

So schelt ich den Rat,	My counsel isn't above criticism,
da schlecht noch dein Ruhm;	because you're far from famous;
denn hohe Güter weiß ich,	there are many advantages
die der Gibichung noch nicht gewann.	the Gibichungs haven't yet attained.

GUNTHER

Verschwiegst du sie,	If you conceal them,
so schelt auch ich.	I'll criticize you too.

HAGEN

In sommerlich reifer Stärke	You're in the prime of life,
seh ich Gibichs Stamm;	but Gibich's line isn't prospering;

ACT 1

[1] With the start of Act 1 proper, the Cycle again commences in the middle of things, explaining as it goes along.

[2] According to Porges (135), Gunther wore a crown in the 1876 Bayreuth premiere.

[3] He's another ruler falling prey to vanity, as we watched Wotan do in *The Rhine Gold*.

dich, Gunther, unbeweibt,	you, Gunther, haven't a wife,
dich, Gutrun', ohne Mann.	you, Gutrune, have never wed.

(Gunther and Gutrune silently think this over.)

GUNTHER

Wen rätst du nun zu frein,	Whom do you want me to woo,
daß unsrem Ruhm es frommt?	so that our fame can flourish?

HAGEN

Ein Weib weiß ich,	I know of a woman
das herrlichste der Welt;	who's matchless in this world;
auf Felsen hoch ihr Sitz;	her home's on a mountaintop,
ein Feuer umbrennt ihren Saal:	with fire surrounding the spot—
nur, wer durch das Feuer bricht,	only a man who breaks through the fire
darf Brünnhildes Freier sein.	can make Brünnhilde his bride.

GUNTHER

Vermag das mein Mut zu bestehn?	Do you feel I have what it takes?

HAGEN

Einem Stärk'ren noch ist's nur bestimmt.	A mightier man is fated for the task.

GUNTHER

Wer ist der streitlichste Mann?	What muscular fellow is that?

HAGEN

Siegfried, der Wälsungen Sproß,	Siegfried, the Wälsungs' son,
der ist der stärkste Held.	is the mighty hero I mean.
Ein Zwillingspaar,	A pair of twins
von Liebe bezwungen,	passionately in love,
Siegmund und Sieglinde,	Siegmund und Sieglinde,
zeugten den echtesten Sohn.	conceived this admirable man.
Der im Walde mächtig erwuchs,	He came of age in the woods,
den wünsch ich Gutrun' zum Mann.	and I want him to wed Gutrune.

GUTRUNE
(Shyly hesitant)

Welche Tat schuf er so tapfer,	What deed did this hero do,
daß als herrlichster Held er genannt?	that people praise him so highly?

HAGEN

Vor Neidhöhle	At Neidhöhle
den Niblungenhort	the Nibelung's gold
bewachte ein riesiger Wurm:	was guarded by a great dragon—

ACT 1

1876 costume design for Gunther by Carl Emil Doepler.

ACT 1

Siegfried schloß ihm den freislichen Schlund, erschlug ihn mit siegendem Schwert. Solch ungeheurer Tat enttagte des Helden Ruhm.	Siegfried closed up its cruel jaws and slew it with his invincible sword. This is the fabled exploit that earned him a hero's fame.

GUNTHER
(Thoughtfully)

Vom Niblungenhort vernahm ich: er birgt den neidlichsten Schatz?	The Nibelung's wealth is notorious— doesn't it add up to an amazing sum?

HAGEN

Wer wohl ihn zu nützen wüßt', dem neigte sich wahrlich die Welt.	If a person put it to work, he could actually subjugate the world.

GUNTHER

Und Siegfried—hat ihn erkämpft?	And Siegfried . . . won it in combat?

HAGEN

Knecht sind die Niblungen ihm.	The Nibelungs are his to command.

GUNTHER

Und Brünnhild' gewänne nur er?	And he alone can capture Brünnhilde?

HAGEN

Keinem andren wiche die Brunst.	Nobody else can cross the flames.

GUNTHER
(Jumping to his feet in exasperation)

Was weckst du Zweifel und Zwist? Was ich nicht zwingen soll, darnach zu verlangen machst du mir Lust?	Why are you stirring up trouble? Why are you tempting me to hope for something I can't ever have?

(He strides angrily back and forth around the villa. Hagen, still seated, stops him in mid-circuit and motions him aside with a secretive gesture.)

HAGEN

Brächte Siegfried die Braut dir heim, wär' dann nicht Brünnhilde dein?	What if Siegfried won the bride, then handed Brünnhilde to you?

GUNTHER
(Turning away, even more skeptical)

Was zwänge den frohen Mann für mich die Braut zu frein?	How could I coerce that carefree warrior to give me a girl he'll woo?

ACT 1

1876 costume design for Gutrune by Carl Emil Doepler.

ACT 1

HAGEN
(Still seated)

Ihn zwänge bald deine Bitte—	You could coerce him . . .
bänd' ihn Gutrun' zuvor.	if he came to love Gutrune.

GUTRUNE

Du Spötter, böser Hagen!	O mocking, malicious Hagen!
Wie sollt' ich Siegfried binden?	Why would Siegfried want me?
Ist er der herrlichste	If he's the mightiest
Held der Welt,	warrior in the world,
der Erde holdeste Frauen	the earth's most enchanting women
friedeten längst ihn schon.	have long since enjoyed his love.

HAGEN
(Whispering in Gutrune's ear)

Gedenk des Trankes im Schrein;   Remember that potion in the chest;

(Confidentially)

vertraue mir, der ihn gewann:	I procured it, and trust me— [1]
den Helden, des du verlangst,	it will force any hero you fancy
bindet er liebend an dich.	to fall in love with you.

(Gunther has come back to the table and is listening in.)

Träte nun Siegfried ein,	If Siegfried turned up and sipped
genöß' er des würzigen Tranks—	that potion made from medicinal plants,
daß vor dir ein Weib er ersah,	he'd forget every woman but you,
daß je ein Weib ihm genaht,	every female he knew in the past
vergessen müßt' er des ganz.	would fade from his memory. [2]
Nun redet:	Let me hear—
wie dünkt euch Hagens Rat?	how do you like Hagen's plan?

GUNTHER
(Exultantly)

Gepriesen sei Grimhild',	Bless Lady Grimhilde
die uns den Bruder gab!	for giving us such a brother!

GUTRUNE

Möcht' ich Siegfried je ersehn!   I can't wait to see Siegfried!

GUNTHER

Wie fänden wir ihn auf?   Where do we search for him?

(A horn call is audible upstage audience left. Hagen listens to it. He turns to Gunther.)

HAGEN

Jagt er auf Taten	As he looks for adventure
wonnig umher,	in his lighthearted way,
zum engen Tann	a little forest of firs

ACT 1

[1] Procured it from whom? Mime?

[2] Note that Hagen doesn't claim Siegfried will lose *other* memories, just those pertaining to women (i.e., Brünnhilde in particular).

ACT 1

wird ihm die Welt:	is what the world is to him—
wohl stürmt er in rastloser Jagd	in his hunting he'll surely roam
auch zu Gibichs Strand an den Rhein.	as far as Gibich's home on the Rhine.

GUNTHER

Willkommen hieß' ich ihn gern.   I'll be happy to welcome him.

(There's another horn call, closer but still far off. Both men listen. Hagen runs down to the shore.)

Vom Rhein her tönt das Horn.   I heard a horn call out on the river.

HAGEN
(Looking downstream and shouting back)

In einem Nachen Held und Roß!	It's a hero and his horse on a barge!
Der bläst so munter das Horn!	He blew that boisterous horn call!

(Gunther goes halfway down, then stops to listen.)

Ein gemächlicher Schlag	With leisurely strokes
wie von müßiger Hand,	and a lazy ease,
treibt jach den Kahn	he's propelling the craft
wider den Strom:	against the current—
so rüstiger Kraft	such carefree power
in des Ruders Schwung	in piloting his boat
rühmt sich nur der,	means he must be
der den Wurm erschlug.	the dragonslayer himself.
Siegfried ist es, sicher kein Andrer!	It's definitely Siegfried out there!

GUNTHER

Jagt er vorbei?   Is he going on by?

HAGEN
(Cupping his hands and calling to the barge)

Hoiho! Wohin,	Hoiho! Where are
du heit'rer Held?	you heading, good hero?

SIEGFRIED'S VOICE
(Far off)

Zu Gibichs starkem Sohne.   To Gibich's mighty son.

HAGEN

Zu seiner Halle entbiet ich dich.   This is his villa, pay us a visit.

(Siegfried and his barge approach shore.)

Hieher! Hier lege an!   Over here! Put in here!

(Siegfried puts in. Hagen makes the barge fast with a chain. Siegfried jumps ashore with his horse.)

ACT 1

1876 costume design for Gunther by Carl Emil Doepler.

Scene 2

HAGEN

Heil! Heil Siegfried, teurer Held!	Greetings! Greetings, Siegfried, sweet hero! [1]

(Gunther is down on the riverbank by Hagen. Still on her throne, Gutrune looks at Siegfried in awed admiration. Gunther's expression is one of warm welcome. For a moment everybody stands and stares.)

SIEGFRIED
(Hand on his horse and motionless by the barge)

Wer ist Gibichs Sohn?	Which of you is Gibich's son?

GUNTHER

Gunther, ich, den du suchst.	I'm Gunther, the man you seek.

SIEGFRIED

Dich hört' ich rühmen	You've quite a reputation
weit am Rhein:	along the Rhine—
nun ficht mit mir,	on guard, and reveal
oder sei mein Freund!	if you're friend or foe!

GUNTHER

Laß den Kampf!	No need for weapons!
Sei willkommen!	Welcome to my home!

SIEGFRIED
(Looking calmly around)

Wo berg ich mein Roß?	Where do I stable my horse?

HAGEN

Ich biet ihm Rast.	I'll find him a stall.

SIEGFRIED
(Facing Hagen)

Du riefst mich Siegfried:	You called me Siegfried—
sahst du mich schon?	have we met before?

HAGEN

Ich kannte dich nur	Your mighty strength
an deiner Kraft.	showed who you were.

SIEGFRIED
(Turning his horse over to Hagen)

Wohl hüte mir Grane:	Take good care of Grane—
du hieltest nie	you've never held
von edlerer Zucht	the reins of
am Zaume ein Roß.	a more regal horse.

ACT 1

[1] Hagen sings this welcome to the motif of Alberich's curse on the ring:

Siegfried the mighty hero.
IN AN 1882 ILLUSTRATION
BY HOWARD PYLE

ACT 1

(Hagen leads the horse off. Siegfried keeps a watchful eye on it and doesn't notice Hagen's discreet signal to Gutrune, who enters the door to her room at audience left. Gunther strides over to Siegfried and ushers him into the villa.)

GUNTHER

Begrüße froh, o Held,	A hearty welcome, good hero,
die Halle meines Vaters:	to the home of my fathers—
wohin du schreitest,	everywhere you walk,
was du ersiehst,	all that you witness,
das achte nun dein Eigen;	look on it as your own;
dein ist mein Erbe,	my heritage is yours,
Land und Leut':	my lands and yeomen—
hilf, mein Leib, meinem Eide!	here's my hand, I give you my oath!
Mich selbst geb ich zum Mann.	I'm completely at your command.

SIEGFRIED

Nicht Land noch Leute biete ich,	I haven't any lands or lackeys,
noch Vaters Haus und Hof:	no house or farm from my fathers—
einzig erbt' ich	the property I was granted
den eig'nen Leib—	is my own person . . .
lebend zehr ich den auf.	which grows older by the day.
Nur ein Schwert hab ich,	Otherwise I've a weapon
selbst geschmiedet:	that I forged myself—
hilf, mein Schwert, meinem Eide!	and it will faithfully witness my oath!
Das biet ich mit mir zum Bund.	I swear we're both at your service.

HAGEN
(Returning and standing behind Siegfried.)

Doch des Niblungenhortes	But aren't the Nibelung's riches
nennt die Märe dich Herrn?	rumored to be yours as well?

SIEGFRIED
(Turning to Hagen)

Des Schatzes vergaß ich fast;	The treasure slipped my mind,
so schätz ich sein müß'ges Gut!	it means so little to me!
In einer Höhle ließ ich's liegen,	I left the gold down in a cave
wo ein Wurm es einst bewacht.	where a dragon once guarded it.

HAGEN

Und nichts entnahmst du ihm?	You didn't take anything?

SIEGFRIED

Dies Gewirk, unkund seiner Kraft.	This trinket, whatever it is.

HAGEN

Den Tarnhelm kenn ich,	That's called a tarnhelmet,
der Niblungen künstliches Werk:	the Nibelung's cleverest creation—
er taugt, bedeckt er dein Haupt,	if you don this device,

ACT 1

Design sketch by Josef Hoffmann: Act 1 of *Twilight for the Gods* at its 1876 Bayreuth premiere.

ACT 1

dir zu tauschen jede Gestalt;	you can turn into any shape;
verlangt dich's an fernsten Ort,	also you can travel long distances
er entführt flugs dich dahin.	in the twinkling of an eye. [1]
Sonst nichts entnahmst du dem Hort?	You took nothing else of the treasure?

SIEGFRIED

Einen Ring.   Simply a ring.

HAGEN

Den hütest du wohl?   You have it in safekeeping?

SIEGFRIED
(Softly)

Den hütet ein hehres Weib.   It's in the hands of a heavenly woman.

HAGEN
(To himself)

Brünnhild'!   Brünnhilde!

GUNTHER

Nicht, Siegfried, sollst du mir tauschen.	No need, Siegfried, to share your treasures.
Tand gäb' ich für dein Geschmeid,	It wouldn't be a fair exchange
nähmst all mein Gut du dafür:	if you took my entire fortune—
ohn' Entgelt dien ich dir gern.	I serve you gladly, no need for gifts.

(Hagen now holds Gutrune's door open. Gutrune comes through it carrying a filled drinking horn, which she brings to Siegfried.)

GUTRUNE

Willkommen, Gast,	Welcome, dear guest,
in Gibichs Haus!	to the house of Gibich!
Seine Tochter reicht dir den Trank.	His daughter hands you this drink.

SIEGFRIED
*(He bows courteously to her and takes the horn.
Holding it thoughtfully, he sings in a hushed voice.)*

Vergäß' ich Alles,	If I lost the memory
was du mir gabst,	of all you taught me,
von einer Lehre	one lesson
laß ich doch nie:	would still be left—
den ersten Trunk	I dedicate this toast
zu treuer Minne,	to our true love,
Brünnhilde, bring ich dir!	and drink it to you, Brünnhilde!

(He lifts the horn and takes a long drink. He gives the horn back to Gutrune, who lowers her eyes, flustered and ashamed. Siegfried suddenly stares at her with blazing passion.)

Die so mit dem Blitz	My sight is scorched
den Blick du mir sengst,	by the look in your eyes,
was senkst du dein Auge vor mir?	why do you lower them before me?

ACT 1

[1] A property of the tarnhelmet that
the Cycle didn't share with us earlier.

The potion of forgetfulness.
FROM AN 1882 ILLUSTRATION
BY THEODOR PIXIS

ACT 1

(Gutrune raises them, cheeks crimson. He responds ardently.)

Ha, schönstes Weib!	Oh, you stunning maiden!
Schließe den Blick;	Shut them once more;
das Herz in der Brust	the heart in my chest
brennt mir sein Strahl,	is charred by their heat,
zu feurigen Strömen fühl ich	I feel their fiery radiance
ihn zehrend zünden mein Blut!	rush boiling through my blood!

(His voice quivering)

Gunther, wie heißt deine Schwester?	Gunther, what's your sister's name?

GUNTHER

Gutrune.	Gutrune.

SIEGFRIED
(Quietly)

Sind's gute Runen,	Are they good runes
die ihrem Aug' ich entrate?	I'm reading in her eyes?

(He impetuously seizes Gutrune's hand.)

Deinem Bruder bot ich mich zum Mann;	I swore to serve your brother;
der Stolze schlug mich aus;	he proudly put me off;
trügst du, wie er, mir Übermut,	would you mistreat me as harshly,
böt' ich mich dir zum Bund?	if I sought your hand in marriage?

(Gutrune can't help exchanging glances with Hagen; she bows meekly as if she felt undeserving, then leaves the room with unsteady steps. Siegfried gazes after her, spellbound; Hagen and Gunther eye him all the while. Siegfried speaks without turning around.)

Hast du, Gunther, ein Weib?	Are you married, Gunther?

GUNTHER

Nicht freit' ich noch,	I haven't a mate as yet,
und einer Frau	but the woman I want
soll ich mich schwerlich freun:	is too hard for me to woo—
auf Eine setzt' ich den Sinn,	I've set my mind on a maiden
die kein Rat mir je gewinnt.	but have no way of winning her.

SIEGFRIED
(Turning heartily to Gunther)

Was wär' dir versagt,	What could be too hard,
steh ich zu dir?	if you have my help?

GUNTHER

Auf Felsen hoch ihr Sitz—	Her home's on a mountaintop . . .

ACT 1

"Oh, you stunning maiden!"
(1911 WATERCOLOR BY ARTHUR RACKHAM)

ACT 1

SIEGFRIED
(Startled and instantly interrupting)

—auf Felsen hoch ihr Sitz?	. . . her home's on a mountaintop?

GUNTHER

ein Feuer umbrennt den Saal.—	. . . with fire surrounding the spot.

SIEGFRIED

—ein Feuer umbrennt den Saal?	. . . with fire surrounding the spot?

GUNTHER

Nur wer durch das Feuer bricht—	Only a man who breaks through the fire . . .

SIEGFRIED
(Struggling to recall some lost memory)

—Nur wer durch das Feuer bricht?	. . . only a man who breaks through the fire?

GUNTHER

darf Brünnhildes Freier sein.	. . . can make Brünnhilde his bride.

(At the mention of Brünnhilde's name, Siegfried's facial expression shows he has no memory of her whatever.) [1]

Nun darf ich den Fels nicht erklimmen,	I dare not fare onto that mountain,
das Feuer verglimmt mir nie!	the fire won't die down for me!

SIEGFRIED
(Leaving his ruminations and turning cheerily to Gunther)

Ich fürchte kein Feuer,	I'm not frightened of any fire,
für dich frei ich die Frau:	and I'll woo the woman for you—
denn dein Mann bin ich,	I'm at your service
und mein Mut ist dein,	and my skills are yours,
gewinn ich mir Gutrun' zum Weib.	if I can wed Gutrune as well.

GUNTHER

Gutrune gönn ich dir gerne.	I'll gladly grant you Gutrune.

SIEGFRIED

Brünnhilde bring ich dir!	Then I'll bring you Brünnhilde!

GUNTHER

Wie willst du sie täuschen?	How will you trick her?

SIEGFRIED

Durch des Tarnhelms Trug	With the tarnhelmet's magic
tausch ich mir deine Gestalt.	I'll take on your appearance. [2]

ACT 1

[1] But he'll keep his other memories. In Acts 2 and 3 he'll readily recall his youthful adventures with Mime, Fafner, and the Wanderer.

[2] Siegfried's showing a new aptitude for deception. Gibichung influence?

ACT 1

GUNTHER

So stelle Eide zum Schwur!	Let's seal our bargain with an oath!

SIEGFRIED

Blutbrüderschaft	We'll swear to be blood brothers
schwöre ein Eid!	with the oath we take!

(Hagen pours new wine into a drinking horn; he holds it out to Siegfried and Gunther, who nick their forearms with their swords, then hold them over the drinking horn. While Hagen keeps it between them, both men place two fingers on it.) [1]

Blühenden Lebens	The lively bloom
labendes Blut	of my life blood
träufelt' ich in den Trank.	is dripping into this drink.

GUNTHER

Bruder-brünstig	Brotherly bravery
mutig gemischt,	makes this brew,
blüh im Trank unser Blut.	mixing and blending our blood.

BOTH

Treue trink ich dem Freund!	I drink in devotion to my friend!
Froh und frei	In freedom and delight
entblühe dem Bund	may this partnership blossom
Blutbrüderschaft heut!	from our pact as blood brothers!

GUNTHER

Bricht ein Bruder den Bund,	If a brother breaks his word . . .

SIEGFRIED

Trügt den Treuen der Freund:	if he's false to his friend—

BOTH

Was in Tropfen heut	. . . the drops that now
hold wir tranken,	nurture this drink
in Strahlen ström' es dahin,	will flow in rivers
fromme Sühne dem Freund!	to righteously repay that friend!

GUNTHER
(Drinking and handing the horn to Siegfried.)

So biet ich den Bund!	Thus I'm part of this pact!

SIEGFRIED

So—	Thus . . .

(Drinking and handing the empty horn to Hagen)

trink ich dir Treu!	. . . I drink in devotion to you!

ACT 1

[1] During this ceremony the orchestra keeps repeating the motif associated with Wotan's protection of oaths and agreements:

The god's regime has ended, but its ideals of truth telling and fair dealing live on.

ACT 1

(Hagen chops the horn in two with his sword. Gunther and Siegfried shake hands. Siegfried looks over at Hagen, who stood behind him during the ceremony.)

Was nahmst du am Eide nicht teil?	Why didn't you participate in the oath?

HAGEN

Mein Blut verdürb' euch den Trank;	My blood would debase your drink;
nicht fließt mir's echt	it isn't patrician
und edel wie euch:	and pure like yours—
störrisch und kalt	it's stubborn, cold,
stockt's in mir,	slow to circulate,
nicht will's die Wange mir röten.	and puts no color in my cheeks.
Drum bleib ich fern	I stay far away
vom feurigen Bund.	from such fiery pacts. [1]

GUNTHER
(To Siegfried)

Laß den unfrohen Mann!	Forget the gloomy fellow!

SIEGFRIED
(Picking his shield back up)

Frisch auf die Fahrt!	Not a second to lose!
Dort liegt mein Schiff:	My boat's set to leave—
schnell führt es zum Felsen.	we'll soon make it to the mountain.

(He whispers his plan to Gunther)

Eine Nacht am Ufer	You'll wait overnight
harrst du im Nachen;	below in the barge;
die Frau fährst du dann heim.	then you'll bring the woman home.

(He turns to go and motions Gunther to follow him.)

GUNTHER

Rastest du nicht zuvor?	Wouldn't you rather rest a while?

SIEGFRIED

Um die Rückkehr ist's mir jach.	I'm eager to return for my reward.

(He heads to the riverbank to cast off the boat.)

GUNTHER

Du, Hagen! Bewache die Halle!	Hagen! Keep watch over our home!

(He follows Siegfried to the shore. Stowing their weapons on board, Siegfried and Gunther hoist sail and cast off; meanwhile Hagen picks up his spear and shield. Gutrune appears in the doorway of her room just as Siegfried propels the barge out to midriver.)

GUTRUNE

Wohin eilen die Schnellen?	Where are they speeding off to?

ACT 1

[1] Note that though he didn't take part in the oath, he administered it. This won't be the only time he assumes that function during Day 3.

ACT 1

HAGEN
(Taking a leisurely seat in front of the villa with his shield and spear)

Zu Schiff—Brünnhild' zu frei'n.	They're sailing . . . to woo Brünnhilde.

GUTRUNE

Siegfried?	Siegfried?

HAGEN

Sieh, wie's ihn treibt,	See how much he wants
zum Weib dich zu gewinnen.	to make you his wife.

GUTRUNE

Siegfried—mein!	Siegfried—mine!

(She excitedly returns to her room. Siegfried propels the barge downstream and out of sight.)

HAGEN
(Sitting motionless, his back against the jamb of the villa's front door) [1]

Hier sitz ich zur Wacht,	I sit on watch and wait,
wahre den Hof,	vigilantly guarding
wehre die Halle dem Feind.	the grounds and villa from foes.
Gibichs Sohne	Gibich's son
wehet der Wind,	sails before the wind
auf Werben fährt er dahin.	to seek a wife for himself.
Ihm führt das Steuer	Piloting his course
ein starker Held,	is a powerful hero
Gefahr ihm will er bestehn:	who'll handle the perils in his place—
die eig'ne Braut	that hero will bring
ihm bringt er zum Rhein;	his own bride to the Rhine;
mir aber bringt er den Ring!	but to me he'll bring the ring!
Ihr freien Söhne,	You merry fellows
frohe Gesellen,	were born as free men,
segelt nur lustig dahin!	laugh away as you sail along!
Dünkt er euch niedrig,	Though you look down on me,
ihr dient ihm doch,	you'll serve me soon—
des Niblungen Sohn.	I'm the Nibelung's son. [2]

(A curtain in front of the villa closes, cutting off the audience's view of the stage.)

ACT 1

[1] The orchestra ushers in this soliloquy with a short, stark, gruesome motif:

Throughout Day 3 it will be associated with Hagen's scheming.

[2] Only now does the Cycle identify this individual. Many productions do so prematurely. We were told in Act 2 of *The Valkyrie* that Alberich had slept with a human woman and sired a son to help him regain the ring. Now we learn that Lady Grimhilde was the woman, Hagen their son. The Cycle doesn't say if she was Lord Gibich's wife at the time.

It's the dark elves who are hatching the macabre scheme currently in progress. Wotan pulled the strings during Day 1; now it's Alberich's turn.

ACT 1

Scene 3

(The curtain opens again on the same mountain setting as in the Prologue. Brünnhilde is seated by the cave opening and silently admiring Siegfried's ring. Full of happy memories, she covers the ring with kisses. There's a thunderclap in the distance; she looks around and listens. She returns to the ring. Lightning flashes. Brünnhilde listens again, looks into the distance, and spies a dark storm cloud sweeping toward the cliff edge.)

BRÜNNHILDE

Altgewohntes Geräusch	Noises once familiar to me
raunt meinem Ohr die Ferne.	fall on my ears from far away.
Ein Luftroß jagt	A sky horse is speeding
im Laufe daher;	across the heavens;
auf der Wolke fährt es	it's coming through the clouds
wetternd zum Fels.	toward this mountain.
Wer fand mich Einsame auf?	Who's making contact with me?

WALTRAUTE'S VOICE
(Far off)

Brünnhilde! Schwester!	Brünnhilde! Sister!
Schläfst oder wachst du?	Are you sleeping or awake?

BRÜNNHILDE
(Instantly on her feet)

Waltrautes Ruf,	It's Waltraute speaking,
so wonnig mir kund!	what a delightful surprise!

(Calling to her)

Kommst du Schwester?	What brings you, sister?
Schwingst dich kühn zu mir her?	Why were you brave enough to fly here?

(She runs to the cliff edge.)

Dort im Tann—	There in the fir trees—
—dir noch vertraut—	you haven't forgotten—
steige vom Roß	leave your racehorse
und stell den Renner zur Rast!	and let him rest!

(She dashes into the fir trees, where a loud noise like a thunderclap rings out. Brünnhilde excitedly comes back with her sister; in her delight she doesn't notice that Waltraute is quivering with anxiety.)

Kommst du zu mir?	You're visiting me?
Bist du so kühn,	You're valiant enough
magst ohne Grauen	to face down your fears
Brünnhild bieten den Gruß?	and meet with me once more?

ACT 1

Full of happy memories, she covers the ring with kisses.
1911 WATERCOLOR BY ARTHUR RACKHAM

ACT 1

WALTRAUTE

Einzig dir nur	You're the only reason
galt meine Eil'.	I've rushed here.

BRÜNNHILDE
(Bursting with happiness and excitement)

So wagtest du, Brünnhild' zulieb,	So for Brünnhilde's sake you dared
Walvaters Bann zu brechen?	to disobey Father of the Slain?
Oder wie—o sag!—	Or—tell me the truth—
wär' wider mich	have I've gotten back
Wotans Sinn erweicht?	into Wotan's good graces?
Als dem Gott entgegen	I defied the god
Siegmund ich schützte,	when I defended Siegmund,
fehlend—ich weiß es—	which was a crime—I know—
erfüllt' ich doch seinen Wunsch.	yet I carried out his actual wishes.
Daß sein Zorn sich verzogen,	But his anger with me abated,
weiß ich auch.	which I also know.
Denn verschloß er mich gleich in Schlaf,	Though he cast a sleeping spell on me,
fesselt' er mich auf dem Fels,	then confined me on this mountain
wies er dem Mann mich zur Magd,	so I'd be at the mercy of any man
der am Weg mich fänd' und erweckt—	who wandered by and woke me,
meiner bangen Bitte	he did me the favor
doch gab er Gunst:	I begged in my fear—
mit zehrendem Feuer	he surrounded this summit
umzog er den Fels,	with scorching flames
dem Zagen zu wehren den Weg.	to frighten off the fainthearted.
So zur Seligsten	So I profited infinitely
schuf mich die Strafe:	from this punishment—
der herrlichste Held	an incomparable hero
gewann mich zum Weib!	won me for his wife!
In seiner Liebe	Thanks to his love,
leucht und lach ich heut auf!	I live today in laughter and delight!

(She hugs Waltraute while the latter nervously resists.)

Lockte dich Schwester mein Los?	Are you drawn by my destiny, sister?
An meiner Wonne	You'd like to join me
willst du dich weiden,	in my joyful existence
teilen, was mich betraf?	and experience it too?

WALTRAUTE
(Harshly)

Teilen den Taumel,	Experience your frenzies,
der dich Törin erfaßt?	you foolish woman?
Ein Andres bewog mich in Angst,	I fear that something else spurs me
zu brechen Wotans Gebot.	to defy Wotan's decree. [1]

(Surprised, Brünnhilde finally notices Waltraute's agitation.)

ACT 1

Sky horse speeding along.
FROM A 1913 PAINTING BY
HERMANN HENDRICH

[1] When we first met her in Act 3 of *The Valkyrie*, Waltraute was a humble sentry. Now she's taking initiative and assuming a leadership role.

ACT 1

BRÜNNHILDE

Angst und Furcht	You poor dear, you're
fesseln dich Arme?	full of fear and dread?
So verzieh der Strenge noch nicht?	So the pitiless god hasn't pardoned me?
Du zagst vor des Strafenden Zorn?	You're afraid you'll be angrily punished?

WALTRAUTE
(Grimly)

Dürft' ich ihn fürchten,	If I had such fears,
meiner Angst fänd' ich ein End!	I wouldn't be feeling so anxious!

BRÜNNHILDE

Staunend versteh ich dich nicht.	I'm confused and don't understand.

WALTRAUTE

Wehre der Wallung,	Come to your senses
achtsam höre mich an!	and listen carefully!
Nach Walhall wieder	The fear that draws me
treibt mich die Angst,	back to Valhalla
die von Walhall hierher mich trieb.	also drives me here to you.

BRÜNNHILDE
(Startled)

Was ist's mit den ewigen Göttern?	What's troubling the timeless gods?

WALTRAUTE

Höre mit Sinn, was ich dir sage!	Listen closely and you'll learn!
Seit er von dir geschieden,	After you and he separated,
zur Schlacht nicht mehr	Wotan didn't send us back
schickte uns Wotan:	into battle anymore—
irr und ratlos	lost and leaderless,
ritten wir ängstlich zu Heer;	our entire band floundered in fear;
Walhalls mutige Helden	Valhalla's noble heroes
mied Walvater.	were likewise neglected.
Einsam zu Roß,	Riding his steed,
ohne Ruh noch Rast,	without rest or respite,
durchschweift' er als Wandrer die Welt.	he roamed the world as a solitary Wanderer.
Jüngst kehrte er heim;	Recently he returned home;
in der Hand hielt er	he held in his hands
seines Speeres Splitter,	the remains of his spear,
die hatte ein Held ihm geschlagen,	which a hero had split in two. [1]
Mit stummem Wink	He silently sent
Walhalls Edle	Valhalla's warriors
wies er zum Forst,	into the forest
die Weltesche zu fällen.	to fell the World Ash Tree.
Des Stammes Scheite	The logs from its trunk
hieß er sie schichten	he had them heap
zu ragendem Hauf	in a lofty pile

ACT 1

[1] So this event on Day 2 took place "recently" *(jüngst)*, suggesting that Brünnhilde and Siegfried are still relatively youthful and naïve—an inference supported later by the ease with which the dark elves deceive them both.

Some may feel, however, that "questions of time are irrelevant in a mythological context." (Spencer et al. 371, n. 163).

rings um der Seligen Saal.	around our holy palace.
Der Götter Rat	He called the gods
ließ er berufen;	into conference;
den Hochsitz nahm	he sat on his throne
heilig er ein:	with a solemn air—
ihm zu Seiten	on both sides of him
hieß er die Bangen sich setzen,	his trembling brethren took their seats,
in Ring und Reih'	ringed by rows
die Hall' erfüllen die Helden.	of heroes throughout the throne room.
So sitzt er,	And there he sits,
sagt kein Wort,	not saying a thing,
auf hehrem Sitze	on his stately throne,
stumm und ernst,	stern and silent,
des Speeres Splitter	the halves of his spear
fest in der Faust;	clenched in his hand;
Holdas Äpfel	Holda's apples
rührt er nicht an.	hold no appeal for him. [1]
Staunen und Bangen	Confusion and fear
binden starr die Götter.	consume the gods.
Seine Raben beide	He sent out his two ravens
sandt' er auf Reise;	to see what's transpiring;
kehrten die einst	if they return
mit guter Kunde zurück,	and give him good news,
dann noch einmal,	then at last
—zum letzten Mal!—	—and for the last time—
lächelte ewig der Gott.	the god will eternally smile.
Seine Knie umwindend	Clutching his knees,
liegen wir Walküren,	we Valkyries crouch by him,
blind bleibt er	but he's blind
den flehenden Blicken:	to our begging looks—
uns alle verzehrt	all of us are eaten
Zagen und endlose Angst.	with anxiety and endless anguish.
An seine Brust	I held him tight
preßt' ich mich weinend;	and shed many tears;

(Hesitantly)

da brach sich sein Blick,	he relented slightly
er gedachte, Brünnhilde, dein.	when he recalled you, Brünnhilde.
Tief seufzt' er auf,	He heaved a sigh,
schloß das Auge,	shut his eyes,
und wie im Traume	and as if speaking in his sleep,
raunt er das Wort:	whispered these words—
»Des tiefen Rheines Töchtern	"If the Rhine daughters in the depths
gäbe den Ring sie wieder zurück,	were to receive the ring again,
von des Fluches Last	the burden of the curse
erlöst wär' Gott und die Welt!«	would lift from both gods and world!" [2]
Da sann ich nach:	I weighed this—
von seiner Seite,	leaving his side,

ACT 1

[1] He has accepted his mortality.

[2] Some English versions mistranslate these lines to mean that the gods would be "saved," in other words, live on. Wotan isn't saying that.

durch stumme Reihen	I stole away
stahl ich mich fort;	from the silent room;
in heimlicher Hast	swiftly and in secret,
bestieg ich mein Roß,	I straddled my steed
und ritt im Sturme zu dir.	and flew here as fast as I could.
Dich, o Schwester,	Please, dear sister,
beschwör ich nun:	I'm pleading with you—
was du vermagst,	do everything you can,
vollend' es dein Mut;	summon your courage;
ende der Ewigen Qual!	end the gods' suffering!

(She kneels before Brünnhilde.)

BRÜNNHILDE
(Quietly)

Welch banger Träume Mären	What nightmarish tales you're
meldest du Traurige mir!	narrating so tearfully!
Der Götter heiligem	The gods' concerns
Himmelsnebel	high in the clouds
bin ich Törin enttaucht;	are far from my human follies;
nicht faß ich, was ich erfahre.	I don't follow you at all.
Wirr und wüst	Chaos and confusion
scheint mir dein Sinn;	muddy your meaning;
in deinem Aug',	the light in your eyes
so übermüde,	is fading out,
glänzt flackernde Glut.	it's flickering erratically.
Mit blasser Wange,	Your cheeks are white,
du bleiche Schwester,	how wan you look, sister,
was willst du Wilde von mir?	what are you seeking so feverishly?

WALTRAUTE
(Entreating her)

An deiner Hand, der Ring—	The ring you're wearing,
er ist's; hör meinen Rat:	that's all; grant what I ask—
für Wotan wirf ihn von dir!	give it up for Wotan's sake!

BRÜNNHILDE

Den Ring—von mir?	Give up . . . the ring?

WALTRAUTE

Den Rheintöchtern gib ihn zurück!	Return it to the Rhine daughters!

BRÜNNHILDE

Den Rheintöchtern—ich—den Ring?	To the Rhine daughters . . . this ring?
Siegfrieds Liebespfand?	My memento of Siegfried's love?
Bist du von Sinnen?	Have you lost your mind?

ACT 1

"He sent out his two ravens to see what's transpiring."
1911 WATERCOLOR BY ARTHUR RACKHAM

ACT 1

Hör mich, hör meine Angst!
Der Welt Unheil
haftet sicher an ihm.
Wirf ihn von dir,
fort in die Welle!
Walhalls Elend zu enden,
den verfluchten wirf in die Flut!

Ha! weißt du, was er mir ist?
Wie kannst du's fassen,
fühllose Maid!
Mehr als Walhalls Wonne,
mehr als der Ewigen Ruhm
ist mir der Ring:
ein Blick auf sein helles Gold,
ein Blitz aus dem hehren Glanz
gilt mir werter,
als aller Götter
ewig währendes Glück.
Denn selig aus ihm
leuchtet mir Siegfrieds Liebe,
Siegfrieds Liebe!
O, ließ' sich die Wonne dir sagen!
Sie wahrt mir den Reif.
Geh hin zu der Götter
heiligem Rat!
Von meinem Ringe
raune ihnen zu:
Die Liebe ließe ich nie,
mir nähmen nie sie die Liebe,
stürzt' auch in Trümmern
Walhalls strahlende Pracht!

Dies deine Treue?
So in Trauer
entlässest du lieblos die Schwester?

Schwinge dich fort,
fliehe zu Roß!
Den Reif entführst du mir nie!

Wehe! Wehe! Weh dir, Schwester!
Walhalls Göttern weh!

WALTRAUTE
Hear me out, heed my fears!
It will increase
the world's ills.
Get rid of it,
throw it in the river!
End Valhalla's woes,
cast the cursed thing into the waves!

BRÜNNHILDE
What! Can't you see how I prize it?
But how could you,
you callous girl!
It's dearer than Valhalla's glories,
dearer than the gods' renown,
the ring's that precious—
one look at its golden brightness,
one glance at its lustrous brilliance,
means more to me
than the good fortune
of all the gods forever.
It blesses me
with the light of Siegfried's love,
Siegfried's love!
Oh, if only you could grasp its wonders!
This band of gold is my world.
Go back to the gods
in their royal conference!
Concerning my ring,
report this to them—
never will I give up love,
and they'll never take my love away, [1]
even if only dust were left
of Valhalla's dazzling domains!

WALTRAUTE
Are you so disloyal?
Your sister is suffering,
and you selfishly dismiss her?

BRÜNNHILDE
Get back on your horse
and go away!
I'll never give you this band of gold!

WALTRAUTE
You're doomed! You're doomed, sister.
Valhalla's gods are done for!

[1] She sings these lines to the motif in Scene 1 of of *The Rhine Gold* alluding to the denial of love:

But Brünnhilde isn't denying love—she's exulting in it. As the Wanderer reminds us in Act 2 of *Siegfried*, "Everything remains true to itself." Which applies not only to dragons and dwarfs but to someone who cherishes love in its many forms.

ACT 1

(She rushes off. A storm cloud quickly rises from the fir trees.)

BRÜNNHILDE
(Watching the cloud vanish into the distance accompanied by lightning flashes)

Blitzend Gewölk,	And off you storm,
vom Wind getragen,	as swift as the wind,
stürme dahin:	hurrying home—
zu mir nie steure mehr her!	don't head this way again!

(It's now evening. The flames below blaze with greater intensity. Brünnhilde looks serenely over the landscape.)

Abendlich, Dämmern	It's evening, and twilight
deckt den Himmel;	spreads across the skies;
heller leuchtet	the fires below
die hütende Lohe herauf.	are burning more brightly.

(Their fiery glow keeps increasing and reaching higher. Tongues of flame shoot above the cliff edge.)

Was leckt so wütend	Why does the fire whip about
die lodernde Welle zum Wall?	so furiously while it walls me in?
Zur Felsenspitze	It's swamping
wälzt sich der feurige Schwall.	the summit with waves of flame.

(Siegfried's horn sounds in the distance. Overjoyed, Brünnhilde springs to her feet.)

Siegfried!	Siegfried!
Siegfried zurück!	Siegfried's back!
Seinen Ruf sendet er her!	He's blowing his horn call!
Auf! Auf! Ihm entgegen!	I must run to him! Greet him!
In meines Gottes Arm!	Rush into the arms of my god!

(She hurries joyfully to the cliff edge. Waves of flame dart up from below—Siegfried leaps out of them onto a tall outcrop, after which the flames instantly subside and withdraw again to the foot of the mountain. On Siegfried's head is the tarnhelmet, which covers half his face, leaves his eyes visible, and gives him Gunther's appearance.)

Verrat!	I've been betrayed!

(Brünnhilde recoils in shock, retreats downstage, and gazes at Siegfried in speechless amazement.)

Wer drang zu mir?	Who's this intruder?

(Standing motionless on the outcrop upstage, Siegfried leans on his shield and watches Brünnhilde. There's a long silence.)

SIEGFRIED
(Singing in a heavier voice)

Brünnhild'! Ein Freier kam,	Brünnhilde! A suitor's arrived
den dein Feuer nicht geschreckt.	who isn't afraid of your fire.

ACT 1

"Valhalla's gods are done for!"
1911 WATERCOLOR BY ARTHUR RACKHAM

ACT 1

Dich werb ich nun zum Weib:	I'm courting you to be my wife—
du folge willig mir!	come with me now!

BRÜNNHILDE
(Trembling all over)

Wer ist der Mann,	Who's this man
der das vermochte,	who managed to do
was dem Stärksten nur bestimmt?	what was meant only for the mightiest?

SIEGFRIED
(Still not moving)

Ein Held, der dich zähmt,	A hero who'll tame you,
bezwingt Gewalt dich nur.	if I have to take you by force.

BRÜNNHILDE
(Horrified)

Ein Unhold schwang sich	An evil spirit sprang
auf jenen Stein!	onto that outcrop!
Ein Aar kam geflogen,	An eagle flew here
mich zu zerfleischen!	to eat my flesh!
Wer bist du, Schrecklicher!	Who are you, you fearful man?

(Another long silence)

Stammst du von Menschen?	Are you human?
Kommst du von Hellas	Are you part of Hella's
nächtlichem Heer?	underworld host?

SIEGFRIED
(Still motionless, his voice faltering at first, then proceeding more firmly) [1]

Ein Gibichung bin ich,	I'm a Gibichung,
und Gunther heißt der Held,	and Gunther's the hero
dem, Frau, du folgen sollst!	who'll take you home, woman!

BRÜNNHILDE
(Shrieking in desperation)

Wotan! Ergrimmter,	Wotan! You vicious,
grausamer Gott!	vindictive god!
Weh! Nun erseh ich!	Aha! Now I understand
der Strafe Sinn!	your plan to punish me!
Zu Hohn und Jammer	Shame and sorrow
jagst du mich hin!	are to be my sentence!

SIEGFRIED
(Leaping down and walking toward her) [2]

Die Nacht bricht an:	It's dark out now—
in deinem Gemach	we'll enter your dwelling
mußt du dich mir vermählen!	and enjoy our wedding night!

ACT 1

[1] This is the first time we hear Siegfried
tell a lie. Maybe that's why his voice falters.

[2] Meanwhile the orchestra reminds us
us who's in charge here—it repeats the
gruesome motif of Hagen's scheming:

ACT 1

BRÜNNHILDE
(Holding out her finger with Siegfried's ring on it)

Bleib fern! Fürchte dies Zeichen!	Stay away! Heed what this stands for!
Zur Schande zwingst du mich nicht,	You can't drag me into disgrace
so lang der Ring mich beschützt.	as long as this ring shields me.

SIEGFRIED

Mannesrecht gebe er Gunther:	It gives spousal rights to Gunther—
durch den Ring sei ihm vermählt!	it will serve as his wedding ring!

BRÜNNHILDE

Zurück, du Räuber!	Be off, you robber!
Frevelnder Dieb!	You thieving rascal!
Erfreche dich nicht mir zu nahn!	Don't you dare come near me!
Stärker als Stahl	This ring renders me
macht mich der Ring:	stronger than steel—
nie raubst du ihn mir!	you'll never rob me of it!

SIEGFRIED

Von dir ihn zu lösen,	You're taunting me
lehrst du mich nun.	to take it from you.

(He rushes her. They wrestle over it. Brünnhilde breaks loose, flees, and turns at bay. Siegfried seizes her again. She escapes; he overtakes her. They wrestle fiercely. He clutches her hand and pulls the ring from her finger. Brünnhilde screams horribly. As she collapses in his arms, she unwittingly looks into Siegfried's eyes. Siegfried lowers her exhausted body onto a stone bench in front of the cave opening.) [1]

Jetzt bist du mein!	At last you're mine!
Brünnhilde, Gunthers Braut—	You're Gunther's bride, Brünnhilde . . .
gönne mir nun dein Gemach!	now guide me to your bedroom!

BRÜNNHILDE
(Staring blankly, drained and defenseless)

Was könntest du wehren,	How could you help yourself,
elendes Weib!	you hapless woman!

(Siegfried imperiously orders her inside. Trembling, with tottering steps, she goes into the cave. Siegfried draws his sword.)

SIEGFRIED
(Singing in his normal voice)

Nun, Notung, zeuge du,	Now, Notung, bear witness
daß ich in Züchten warb.	that I've wooed honorably.
Die Treue wahrend dem Bruder,	Keep me loyal to my blood brother,
trenne mich von seiner Braut!	let your blade part me from his bride!

(He follows Brünnhilde inside; the curtain closes.)

ACT 1

[1] Surely the most disturbing action sequence in the Cycle—Brünnhilde resists with superheroine strength, but she's up against the era's mightiest warrior. Meanwhile the harsh music repeats motifs associated with Alberich—the motif of the hate underlying his deeds:

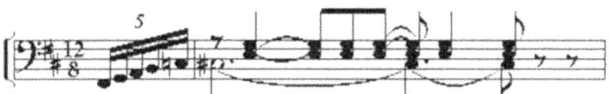

and the motif of the curse the dwarf put on the ring:

As for Siegfried, in the past Mime's lies could goad him to understandable anger, but here he displays the ugly new traits of cold-blooded brutality and macho braggadocio—thanks to the dark elves, their potion, and their tarnhelmet.

ACT 1

LOOKING BACK ON ACT 1

What on earth's happening?
   1) Wotan retires permanently to Valhalla, where the gods are waiting for the end.
   2) The dark elves are starting to direct events, with Hagen their representative.
   3) Siegfried visits the outside world and quickly falls in with evil companions.
   4) He leaves the ring with Brünnhilde behind a fire wall only he can cross.
   5) Hagen and the Gibichungs drug and dupe Siegfried into doing so.
   6) To Brünnhilde the ring's a love token, not a means to power.
   7) Straightaway the ring reverts to its previous owner.

Further forms of love?
   1) Idyllic unreality—Brünnhilde and Siegfried living together in seclusion.
   2) Status seeking—Gunther and Gutrune joining in a disreputable plan to marry up.
   3) Ties of fellowship—Siegfried and Gunther forming a brotherhood pact that overrides all else.
   4) Tribal loyalty—Waltraute sacrificing an individual (Brünnhilde) to save the bloodline (Wotan & Valhalla).

Is Brünnhilde in shock?
   1) Wotan appears to have broken his promise.
   2) A "stranger" penetrates the god's fiery barrier.
   3) The man's eerie and behaves like "an evil spirit."
   4) He's incomparably strong and claims her as his wife.
   5) He assaults her brutally and overpowers her.
   6) He tears off her ring and shares her bed.
   7) He takes her down the mountain as his captive.
   8) These are traumatic experiences.

Why won't the ring protect her?
   1) She doesn't practice any of Alberich's rituals.
   2) She views it as a pledge of love rather than a power symbol.
   3) Actually, the water sprites never promised it would confer invulnerability.
   4) It didn't protect Alberich, Fasolt, or Fafner either.

ACT 1

1876 costume design for Waltraute by Carl Emil Doepler.

ACT 2

ACT 2

Prelude and Scene 1

The curtain opens on the terrace outside the Gibichung villa.

The villa entrance is audience right, the riverbank audience left, its towering rocks furrowed with trails and rising diagonally upstage left. We see an altar stone dedicated to Fricka, above it a bigger one to Wotan, beside it a similar one to Donner. [1] It's night. His spear at hand and his shield beside him, Hagen's asleep in his seat and leaning against the jamb of the villa entrance. The moon appears suddenly and casts a stark light on Hagen and his immediate vicinity. We see Alberich crouching in front of his son, arms on the half-breed's knees.

ALBERICH
(Softly)

Schläfst du, Hagen, mein Sohn?	Are you sleeping, Hagen my son?
Du schläfst und hörst mich nicht,	You're sleeping and can't hear me,
den Ruh' und Schlaf verriet?	whom rest and sleep have forsaken?

HAGEN
(Softly and without moving, so he still seems asleep though his eyes are wide open)

Ich höre dich, schlimmer Albe:	I hear you, evil elf—
was hast du meinem Schlaf zu sagen?	what have you to say while I slumber?

ALBERICH

Gemahnt sei der Macht,	You'll make use of the might
der du gebietest,	at your command,
bist du so mutig,	if you've the character
wie die Mutter dich mir gebar!	of the mother who carried you!

HAGEN
(Still motionless)

Gab mir die Mutter Mut,	If I've my mother's character,
nicht mag ich dir doch danken,	I'm not grateful to her
daß deiner List sie erlag:	for giving in to your trickery— [2]
frühalt, fahl und bleich,	I'm gaunt and gray before my time,
haß ich die Frohen,	hate those who are happy,
freue mich nie!	and am gloomy always!

ALBERICH
(Still crouching)

Hagen, mein Sohn!	Hagen my son!
Hasse die Frohen!	Hate those who are happy!
Mich Lustfreien,	But I, the melancholy,
Leidbelasteten,	miserable dwarf,
liebst du so wie du sollst.	deserve all your love!
Bist du kräftig,	If you've been skillful,

ACT 2

[1] As Act 1 revealed, the gods are waiting passively in Valhalla and have suspended operations. Humans below haven't been informed of the power vacuum, which the dark elves are now busy filling.

[2] In Act 2, Scene 2 of *The Valkyrie*, Wotan describes how Lady Grimhilde prostituted herself: "the Nibelung . . . had his way with a woman, giving her gold for her favors."

ACT 2

kühn und klug,	steadfast, and shrewd,
die wir bekämpfen	the foes we're fighting
mit nächtigem Krieg,	in our nocturnal efforts
schon gibt ihnen Not unser Neid.	have already experienced our envy.
Der einst den Ring mir entriß,	The rascal who nabbed my ring,
Wotan, der wütende Räuber,	Wotan, that rage-filled robber,
vom eig'nen Geschlechte	has been defeated
ward er geschlagen:	by his own descendant—
an den Wälsung verlor er	he conceded to the Wälsung
Macht und Gewalt;	his control and power;
mit der Götter ganzer Sippe	with the gods' entire fellowship
in Angst ersieht er sein Ende.	he anxiously waits for his passing.
Nicht ihn fürcht ich mehr:	I no longer fear him—
fallen muß er mit Allen!	he's doomed to die like everyone else!
Schläfst du, Hagen, mein Sohn?	Are you sleeping, Hagen my son?

HAGEN
(Still not moving)

Der Ewigen Macht,	The deities' power—
wer erbte sie?	who will it pass to?

ALBERICH

Ich—und du!	To me . . . and you!
Wir erben die Welt,	We'll inherit the earth,
trüg ich mich nicht	if I'm correct
in deiner Treu',	in counting on you
teilst du meinen Gram und Grimm.	to share my anger and anguish.
Wotans Speer	Wotan's spear
zerspellte der Wälsung,	was shattered by the Wälsung,
der Fafner, den Wurm,	the dragonslayer
im Kampfe gefällt,	who defeated Fafner,
und kindisch den Reif sich errang;	the lad who laid hold of my ring;
jede Gewalt	he's the possessor
hat er gewonnen:	of all power—
Walhall und Nibelheim	Valhalla and Nibelheim
neigen sich ihm.	are at his command.

(Confidentially)

An dem furchtlosen Helden	But this fearless conquerer
erlahmt selbst mein Fluch;	won't fulfill my curse's conditions;
denn nicht kennt er	he's unaware of
des Ringes Wert,	the ring's uniqueness,
zu nichts nützt er	he doesn't prize
die neidliche Macht.	its coveted power.
Lachend, in liebender Brunst,	Laughing, loving, free of care,
brennt er lebend dahin.	he's frittering his life away.
Ihn zu verderben,	We must destroy him,
taugt uns nun einzig!	that's the only solution!
Schläfst du, Hagen, mein Sohn?	Are you sleeping, Hagen my son?

ACT 2

"I'm not grateful to her for giving in to your trickery."
1911 WATERCOLOR BY ARTHUR RACKHAM

ACT 2

HAGEN
(Still motionless)

Zu seinem Verderben	He'll destroy himself
dient er mir schon.	as he does my bidding.

ALBERICH

Den gold'nen Ring,	That glittering ring,
den Reif—gilt's zu erringen!	the band of gold—get it back!
Ein weises Weib	A wise woman
lebt dem Wälsung zulieb;	lives for the Wälsung's love;
riet es ihm je,	if she guided him
des Rheines Töchtern,	to give it to the Rhine daughters
die in Wassers Tiefen	in the river depths
einst mich betört,	who duped me once,
zurückzugeben den Ring:	the ring would be gone for good—
verloren ging mir das Gold,	its gold would be out of reach,
keine List erlangte es je.	no cunning could capture it again.
Drum, ohne Zögern	So you must hurry
ziel auf den Reif!	and get hold of the ring!
Dich Zaglosen	I bred you
zeugt' ich mir ja,	to be brave
daß wider Helden	and help me fend off
hart du mir hieltest.	my heroic foes.
Zwar—stark nicht genug,	True, you hadn't the strength
den Wurm zu bestehn,	to slay the dragon,
was allein dem Wälsung bestimmt,	which was the Wälsung's destiny alone,
zu zähem Haß doch	but with your stubborn hatred
erzog ich Hagen;	you'll succeed, Hagen;
der soll mich nun rächen,	you'll avenge me
den Ring gewinnen,	and acquire the ring,
dem Wälsung und Wotan zum Hohn!	making a mockery of Wotan and the Wälsung!
Schwörst du mir's, Hagen, mein Sohn?	You swear that to me, Hagen my son?

(From here on out, Alberich begins to fade into the shadows. Signs of dawn appear in the sky.)

HAGEN
(Remaining motionless)

Den Ring soll ich haben;	I'll possess the ring;
harre in Ruh'!	be patient!

ALBERICH

Schwörst du mir's, Hagen, mein Held?	You swear that to me, Hagen my hero?

HAGEN

Mir selbst schwör' ich's;	I swear it to myself;
schweige die Sorge!	set your mind at ease!

ACT 2

"You swear that to me, Hagen my son?"
1911 WATERCOLOR BY ARTHUR RACKHAM

ACT 2

*(During the following Alberich grows less
and less visible, his voice less audible.)*

ALBERICH

Sei treu, Hagen, mein Sohn!	Be loyal, Hagen my son!
Trauter Helde, sei treu!	Hero that I love, be loyal!
Sei treu! Treu!	Be loyal! Loyal!

*(Alberich vanishes completely. [1] Still motionless,
Hagen gazes intently at the Rhine while
the dawning light grows steadily brighter.)*

Scene 2

*(As the sun rises, the river starts to gleam with a reddish hue. Hagen looks up
in surprise as Siegfried suddenly steps out from behind a bush on the bank.)*

SIEGFRIED

Hoiho! Hagen!	Hoiho! Hagen!
Müder Mann!	Sleepyhead!
Siehst du mich kommen?	Didn't you see me coming?

*(Siegfried has resumed his own appearance, though he's still wearing the
tarnhelmet; he takes it off, hangs it from his belt, and strides forward.)*

HAGEN
(Rising in leisurely fashion)

Hei! Siegfried!	Hey, Siegfried!
Geschwinder Helde!	You speedy devil!
Wo brausest du her?	Where'd you drop in from?

SIEGFRIED

Vom Brünnhildenstein;	From Brünnhilde's mountain,
dort sog ich den Atem ein,	where my mouth took the breath
mit dem ich dich rief:	with which I just called to you—
so schnell war meine Fahrt.	I came here as quick as that.
Langsamer folgt mir ein Paar;	The happy couple will take longer,
zu Schiff gelangt das her!	they're traveling by boat.

HAGEN

So zwangst du Brünnhild'?	So you captured Brünnhilde?

SIEGFRIED

Wacht Gutrune?	Isn't Gutrune up?

ACT 2

[1] Music of anguish, gloom, and loneliness has darkened their whole dialogue. Both father and son embody those emotional states: Alberich calls himself a "melancholy, miserable dwarf," Hagen claims he's "gaunt and gray." Their quest for the ring has been painful.

This is our last encounter with Alberich, who hasn't changed since *The Rhine Gold,* has made no progress in self-honesty—of course he's miserable. As for Hagen, he was bred to do his father's dirty work, his filial loyalty has been a lifelong burden—of course he's old before his time.

ACT 2

HAGEN
(Calling into the villa)

Hoiho! Gutrune!	Hoiho! Gutrune!
Komm heraus!	Hurry on out!
Siegfried ist da:	Siegfried's here—
was säumst du drin?	why are you staying inside?

SIEGFRIED
(Facing the villa)

Euch beiden meld ich,	I'll tell you both
wie ich Brünnhild' band.	how I tamed Brünnhilde.

(Gutrune comes out of the villa to greet him)

Heiß mich willkommen,	Give me your warmest welcome,
Gibichskind!	daughter of Gibich!
Ein guter Bote bin ich dir.	I'm the bearer of good news.

GUTRUNE

Freia grüße dich	May Freia bless you
zu aller Frauen Ehre!	on behalf of all women!

SIEGFRIED

Frei und hold	Join with me
sei nun mir Frohem!	in my joy today!
Zum Weib gewann ich dich heut.	I've won you now as my wife!

GUTRUNE

So folgt Brünnhild' meinem Bruder?	So my brother's bringing Brünnhilde?

SIEGFRIED

Leicht ward die Frau ihm gefreit.	I wooed the woman with ease.

GUTRUNE

Sengte das Feuer ihn nicht?	He wasn't scorched by the fire?

SIEGFRIED

Ihn hätt' es auch nicht versehrt;	It didn't even singe him;
doch ich durchschritt es für ihn,	I went through it instead,
da dich ich wollt' erwerben.	because I wanted to win you.

GUTRUNE

Doch dich hat es verschont?	The experience didn't harm you?

SIEGFRIED

Mich freute die schwelende Brunst.	I enjoyed the smoldering heat. [1]

GUTRUNE

Hielt Brünnhild' dich für Gunther?	Did Brünnhilde take you for Gunther?

ACT 2

Gunther's bride.
1913 PORTRAIT OF BRÜNNHILDE
BY HERMANN HENDRICH

[1] Some editions give *schwebende* (gliding, hovering) rather than *schwelende* (smoldering, smoky). The latter seems the better fit. Meanwhile the phrasing again includes *Brünst*, German for "rut," and just as at the close of Day 2, uses fire metaphors to paint Siegfried's sexuality. He's an alpha male.

ACT 2

Ihm glich ich auf ein Haar: der Tarnhelm wirkte das, wie Hagen tüchtig es wies.	**SIEGFRIED** I looked just like him— the tarnhelmet did the trick, as Hagen told us it would.
Dir gab ich guten Rat.	**HAGEN** I gave you good advice.
So zwangst du das kühne Weib?	**GUTRUNE** So you subdued the plucky girl?
Sie wich—Gunthers Kraft.	**SIEGFRIED** She succumbed . . . to Gunther's prowess.
Und—vermählte sie sich dir?	**GUTRUNE** And . . . she lay with you as your wife?
Ihrem Mann gehorchte Brünnhild' eine volle bräutliche Nacht.	**SIEGFRIED** Brünnhilde looked up to her husband throughout her wedding night.
Als ihr Mann doch galtest du?	**GUTRUNE** Weren't you acting as her husband?
Bei Gutrune weilte Siegfried.	**SIEGFRIED** My heart stayed with Gutrune.
Doch zur Seite war ihm Brünnhild'?	**GUTRUNE** But you slept beside Brünnhilde?
Zwischen Ost und West der Nord: so nah—war Brünnhild' ihm fern.	**SIEGFRIED** *(Displaying his sword)* As the north lies between east and west, my blade separated Brünnhilde from me.
Wie empfing Gunther sie nun von dir?	**GUTRUNE** How did you give her to Gunther?
Durch des Feuers verlöschende Lohe im Frühnebel vom Felsen folgte sie mir zu Tal; dem Strande nah, flugs die Stelle tauschte Gunther mit mir: durch des Geschmeides Tugend wünscht' ich mich schnell hierher. Ein starker Wind nun treibt	**SIEGFRIED** Through the fire's dying flames I led her in the morning mist down the mountain to the valley; on the bank below, Gunther promptly traded places with me— using the tarnhelmet's powers, I wished myself here in a twinkling. Now a swift breeze is bringing

ACT 2

Design sketch by Josef Hoffmann: Act 2 of *Twilight for the Gods* at its 1876 Bayreuth premiere.

die Trauten den Rhein herauf.
Drum rüstet jetzt den Empfang!

the sweethearts up the Rhine.
Get ready to receive them!

GUTRUNE

Siegfried! Mächtigster Mann!
Wie faßt mich Furcht vor dir!

Siegfried! Mightiest of men!
I stand in awe of you!

HAGEN
(Calling from the riverbank)

In der Ferne seh ich ein Segel!

I see a sail on the horizon!

SIEGFRIED

So sagt dem Boten Dank!

Thank heavens for the messenger!

GUTRUNE

Lasset uns sie hold empfangen,
daß heiter sie gern hier weile!
Du, Hagen, minnig
rufe die Männer
nach Gibichs Hof zur Hochzeit!
Frohe Frauen
ruf ich zum Fest,
der Freudigen folgen sie gern.

We'll prepare a glorious reception,
and she'll gladly remain with us!
Hagen, give a hearty call
to the clansmen
welcoming them to our joint wedding!
Their women will gladly
join us in Gibich's court
and share in the joyous festivities.

(Heading toward the villa, then looking back at Siegfried)

Rastest du, schlimmer Held?

Ready to relax, you naughty man?

SIEGFRIED

Dir zu helfen—ruh ich aus.

Meeting your needs . . . is my reward. [1]

*(He takes her hand and goes into the villa with her. Hagen climbs
a lofty crag upstage, where he faces out and blows a steerhorn.)*

Scene 3

HAGEN

Hoiho! Hoihohoho!
Ihr Gibichs Mannen,
machet euch auf!
Wehe! Wehe!
Waffen! Waffen!
Waffen durch's Land!
Gute Waffen!
Starke Waffen!
Scharf zum Streit!
Not ist da!
Not! Wehe! Wehe!
Hoiho! Hoihohoho!

Hoiho! Hoihohoho!
Gibichung clansmen,
answer my call!
Battle stations!
To arms! To arms!
To arms, countrymen!
Your best blades!
Strongest blades!
Sharpened for combat! [2]
We need you!
Need you! Battle stations!
Hoiho! Hoihohoho!

ACT 2

[1] This flirty exchange suggests that Gutrune is no longer the mousy, blushing maiden she was in Act 1. Landing a catch like Siegfried has boosted her self-esteem.

[2] Note how quickly Hagen turns the occasion into a red alert. He'll have a crowd of well-armed witnesses to support his scheming.

ACT 2

(Hagen remains on the crag blowing his steerhorn. Other horns reply from various directions. Armed clansmen rush down different trails from the rocky heights, first singly, then in groups. They gather on the riverbank outside the villa.)

CLANSMEN

Was tost das Horn?	Why's the horn sounding?
Was ruft es zu Heer?	Why's it summoning us?
Wir kommen mit Wehr.	We've brought our blades.
Wir kommen mit Waffen.	We're bearing arms.
Hagen! Hagen!	Hagen! Hagen!
Hoiho! Hoiho!	Hoiho! Hoiho!
Welche Not ist da?	Why do you need us?
Welcher Feind ist nah?	What foes are nearby?
Wer gibt uns Streit?	Who's fighting with us?
Ist Gunther in Not?	Is Gunther in need?
Wir kommen mit Waffen.	We've brought our blades.
Mit scharfer Wehr.	They're sharpened for battle.
Hoiho! Ho! Hagen!	Hoiho! Ho! Hagen!

HAGEN
(Still on the crag)

Rüstet euch wohl,	Gather your gear
und rastet nicht!	and remain on guard!
Gunther sollt ihr empfahn:	Get ready to receive Gunther—
ein Weib hat der gefreit.	he wooed a wife for himself.

CLANSMEN

Drohet ihm Not?	Is he in dire need?
Drängt ihn der Feind?	In danger from foes?

HAGEN

Ein freisliches Weib	He's fetched himself
führet er heim.	a formidable woman.

CLANSMEN

Ihm folgen der Magen	Are the men of her family
feindliche Mannen?	In fierce pursuit?

HAGEN

Einsam fährt er,	Nobody's following,
keiner folgt.	he's fine.

CLANSMEN

So bestand er die Not?	So he hasn't any needs?
So bestand er den Kampf?	So he handled things himself?
Sag es an!	Say what happened!

ACT 2

1876 costume designs for Gibichung clansmen by Carl Emil Doepler.

ACT 2

HAGEN

Der Wurmtöter	The dragonslayer
wehrte der Not:	warded off danger—
Siegfried der Held,	Siegfried the warrior
der schuf ihm Heil!	kept him safe!

A CLANSMAN

Was soll ihm das Heer nun noch helfen?	What can our armies do to aid him?

NINE OTHERS

Was hilft ihm nun das Heer?	What aid can our armies give?

HAGEN

Starke Stiere	Bring robust bulls
sollt ihr schlachten;	ripe for the slaughter,
am Weihstein fließe	and spill their blood
Wotan ihr Blut!	on Wotan's altar stone!

A CLANSMAN

Was, Hagen, was heißest du uns dann?	Then what should we do next, Hagen?

EIGHT CLANSMEN

Was heißest du uns dann?	What should we do next?

FOUR OTHERS

Was soll es dann?	What next?

ALL THE CLANSMEN

Was heißest du uns dann?	Then what should we do?

HAGEN

Einen Eber fällen	Slay a boar
sollt ihr für Froh,	as a sacrifice to Froh,
einen stammigen Bock	a sturdy goat
stechen für Donner;	as a gift to Donner,
Schafe aber	and finally sheep
schlachtet für Fricka,	in homage to Fricka,
daß gute Ehe sie gebe!	so she honors the marriage! [1]

(The clansmen start to chuckle.)

TWO CLANSMEN

Schlugen wir Tiere,	After butchering the beasts,
was schaffen wir dann?	what's next on the bill?

ACT 2

[1] As noted, Wotan's regime has ended and the gods are waiting passively in Valhalla. The clansmen, however, don't realize that times have changed, that their sacrifices are obsolete.

But Hagen knows: he slyly mocks Fricka by imitating a sheep's *bah-ah-ah* during the phrase "honors the marriage." Bah indeed.

ACT 2

TEN OTHER CLANSMEN

Schlugen wir Tiere,	After butchering the beasts,
was schaffen wir dann?	what's next on the bill?

HAGEN

Das Trinkhorn nehmt,	Hold the drinking horns
von trauten Frau'n	your darling women
mit Met und Wein	have merrily filled
wonnig gefüllt!	with mead and wine!

ALL THE CLANSMEN

Das Trinkhorn zur Hand,	Drinking horns in hand,
wie halten wir es dann?	how should we behave?

HAGEN

Rüstig gezecht,	Down every drop
bis der Rausch euch zähmt:	till you're totally tipsy—
Alles den Göttern zu Ehren,	all in homage to the gods,
daß gute Ehe sie geben!	so they honor the marriage!

CLANSMEN
(Hooting with laughter)

Groß Glück und Heil	Good luck and good cheer
lacht nun dem Rhein,	light up the Rhine,
da Hagen der Grimme	when surly old Hagen
so lustig mag sein!	is so sweet and benign!
Der Hagedorn	He's a hawthorn bush
sticht nun nicht mehr;	that's no longer prickly;
zum Hochzeitsrufer	they've put him to work
ward er bestellt!	as a wedding planner!

HAGEN
(Back to being serious and coming down from the crag to join the men)

Nun laßt das Lachen,	Now stop your snickering,
mut'ge Mannen!	my courageous clansmen!
Empfangt Gunthers Braut:	Welcome Gunther's bride—
Brünnhilde naht dort mit ihm.	Brünnhilde's on board with him.

(He directs the clansmen to the Rhine; some of them scale the crag, while others stay on the riverbank to greet the arriving barge. He takes some of the clansmen aside.)

Hold seid der Herrin,	Stand by your lady,
helfet ihr treu:	serve her loyally—
traf sie ein Leid,	if she's ever injured,
rasch seid zur Rache!	instantly avenge her! [1]

(He slowly turns and looks upstage. During the following, the boat carrying Gunther and Brünnhilde ascends the Rhine.)

ACT 2

Hagen in court dress.
1871 PAINTING BY FRANZ GAUL

[1] While events unfold, Hagen keeps improvising toward his objectives. Currently he's cultivating the clansmen as allies and observers.

ACT 2

A CLANSMAN
(On the crag)

Heil!	Greetings!

SEVERAL CLANSMEN

Heil!	Greetings!

ANOTHER CLANSMAN

Heil!	Greetings!

(Clansmen stationed higher up now go down to the bank.)

ALL THE CLANSMEN

Willkommen! Willkommen!	Welcome! Welcome!

(Several clansmen rush into the river and tow the barge ashore. Everybody gathers at the water's edge.)

Willkommen, Gunther!	Welcome, Gunther!
Heil! Heil!	Greetings! Greetings!

Scene 4

(Gunther steps off the barge with Brünnhilde; lines of clansmen wait courteously to receive them. During the following Gunther leads Brünnhilde gallantly by the hand.)

CLANSMEN

Heil dir, Gunther!	Hail to you, Gunther!
Heil dir, und deiner Braut!	Hail to you and your bride!
Heil sei Gunther dir	All hail to you, Gunther,
und deiner Braut!	and your bride!
Willkommen!	Welcome!

(They bang their weapons exuberantly.)

GUNTHER
(Introducing the clansmen to Brünnhilde, who looks pale and downcast)

Brünnhild', die hehrste Frau,	Brünnhilde, most regal of women,
bring ich euch her zum Rhein.	now joins us on the banks of the Rhine.
Ein edleres Weib	No man could win
ward nie gewonnen.	a more noble wife.
Der Gibichungen Geschlecht,	The Gibichung race
gaben die Götter ihm Gunst,	has received a gift from the gods,
zum höchsten Ruhm,	so our fame will grow
rag' es nun auf!	and flourish forever!

ACT 2

1876 costume designs for Gutrune's ladies-in-waiting by Carl Emil Doepler.

ACT 2

CLANSMEN
(Saluting by banging their weapons again)

Heil dir,	Hail to you,
glücklicher Gibichung!	happiest of Gibichungs!

(Gunther approaches the villa with Brünnhilde, who continues to look at the ground. [1] Siegfried and Gutrune come outdoors, followed by ladies-in-waiting.)

GUNTHER
(Pausing in front of the villa)

Gegrüßt sei, teurer Held;	Greetings, dear hero;
gegrüßt, holde Schwester!	greetings, darling sister!
Dich seh ich froh ihm zur Seite,	I see you standing gladly beside
der dich zum Weib gewann.	the man who won you as his wife.
Zwei sel'ge Paare	Two happy couples
seh ich hier prangen:	are here at hand—

(He leads Brünnhilde toward them.)

Brünnhild' und Gunther,	Brünnhilde and Gunther,
Gutrun'—und Siegfried!	Gutrune . . . and Siegfried!

(Brünnhilde looks up in shock and sees Siegfried; she stares in amazement. Her hand shakes so violently, Gunther lets go of it; along with everybody else, he's baffled by her reactions.) [2]

SEVERAL CLANSMEN

Was ist ihr? Ist sie entrückt?	What's wrong? Is she delirious?

(Brünnhilde begins to tremble.)

SIEGFRIED
(Taking a step toward Brünnhilde)

Was müht Brünnhildes Blick?	What's bothering Brünnhilde?

BRÜNNHILDE
(Barely coherent)

Siegfried . . . hier? Gutrune . . . ?	Siegfried . . . here? Gutrune. . . ?

SIEGFRIED

Gunthers milde Schwester,	Gunther's sweet sister,
mir vermählt,	now my spouse,
wie Gunther du.	as Gunther is yours.

BRÜNNHILDE
(Suddenly flaring up)

Ich . . . ? Gunther . . . ? Du lügst!	I . . . Gunther. . . ? You lie!

(She staggers and seems about to swoon; Siegfried catches her.)

ACT 2

[1] Observing Brünnhilde's behavior, professionals today might diagnose her as suffering from post-traumatic stress disorder. Don't forget what she experienced at the close of Act 1.

[2] Remember, only *two* of these people know that Siegfried is Brünnhilde's sworn husband: Hagen and Brünnhilde herself. Siegfried doesn't know because of his memory loss, the others because Hagen has concealed the fact.

ACT 2

Mir schwindet das Licht . . .	It's so dark, I can't see . . .

(As he holds her, she feebly looks into Siegfried's eyes.)

Siegfried . . . kennt mich nicht?	Siegfried . . . doesn't recognize me?

SIEGFRIED

Gunther, deinem Weib ist übel!	Gunther, your wife isn't well!

(Pointing to Gunther as he comes over)

Erwache, Frau!	Cheer up, woman!
Hier steht dein Gatte.	Your husband's here.

BRÜNNHILDE

(Seeing the ring on Siegfried's outstretched finger and flaring up a second time)

Ha! . . . Der Ring . . .	What . . . ! The ring . . .
an seiner Hand!	on his hand! [1]
Er . . . ? Siegfried . . . ?	He . . . ? Siegfried . . . ?

SEVERAL CLANSMEN

Was ist? Was ist?	What's wrong? What's wrong?

HAGEN

(Upstage, circulating among the clansmen)

Jetzt merket klug,	Pay attention
was die Frau euch klagt!	to her accusations! [2]

BRÜNNHILDE

(Trying to calm her agitation and regain her self-control)

Einen Ring sah ich	That ring I see
an deiner Hand:	on your finger there—
nicht dir gehört er,	it isn't yours,
ihn entriß mir—	it was snatched from me . . .

(Indicating Gunther)

dieser Mann.	by this fellow.
Wie mochtest von ihm	How could you have
den Ring du empfah'n?	come by that ring?

SIEGFRIED

(Pensively studying the ring on his finger)

Den Ring empfing ich	The ring didn't come
nicht von ihm.	from him. [3]

BRÜNNHILDE

(To Gunther)

Nahmst du von mir den Ring,	If you took that ring from me
durch den ich dir vermählt,	to serve as your wedding band,
so melde ihm dein Recht,	then say you've a right to it,
ford're zurück das Pfand!	tell him you want it back!

ACT 2

[1] Oops, he didn't give Gunther the ring. Events may have moved too quickly for this novice intriguer: wearing both the ring and Gunther's form, he hustled Brünnhilde down to the river, vanished back to the villa, and left the real Gunther to take over—minus the ring.

In any case the band of gold is now closer to its actual home than at any time since the start of the Cycle. It's been a long, twisting road.

[2] Hagen is priming potential witnesses. Under this next sequence, as at the close of Act 1, the orchestra will repeat motifs associated with the dark elves—the motif of the hatred that underlies Alberich's deeds:

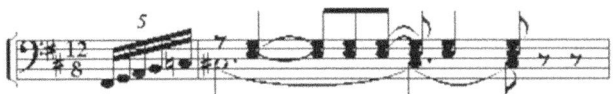

and the motif of the dwarf's bitter curse on the ring:

[3] So far, he's telling the truth.

ACT 2

GUNTHER
(Thoroughly puzzled)

Den Ring . . . ? Ich gab ihm keinen:	That ring? I gave him no such thing—
doch—kennst du ihn auch gut?	but . . . is it the one you think?

BRÜNNHILDE

Wo bärgest du den Ring,	Where did the ring go
den du von mir erbeutet?	that you got from me?

(Gunther doesn't know what to say. [1]
Brünnhilde turns furiously to Siegfried.)

Ha! Dieser war es,	Aha! He's the one
der mir den Ring entriß:	who took the ring—
Siegfried, der trugvolle Dieb!	Siegfried's a treacherous thief!

*(Everybody looks breathlessly at Siegfried,
who's intently studying the ring.)*

SIEGFRIED

Von keinem Weib	This band of gold
kam mir der Reif,	came from no woman,
noch war's ein Weib,	nor was it booty
dem ich ihn abgewann:	I won from a woman— [2]
genau erkenn ich	I recognize it now
des Kampfes Lohn,	as the reward I earned
den vor Neidhöhl' einst ich bestand,	when I visited Neidhöhle once
als den starken Wurm ich erschlug.	and vanquished a dreadful dragon. [3]

HAGEN
(Stepping between them)

Brünnhild', kühne Frau!	Brünnhilde, brave woman!
Kennst du genau den Ring?	Do you recognize this ring?
Ist's der, den du Gunther gabst,	If you gave it to Gunther,
so ist er sein,	it's his property
und Siegfried gewann ihn durch Trug,	and Siegfried got it by trickery,
den der Treulose büßen sollt'!	so the traitor must pay!

BRÜNNHILDE
(Shrieking in dreadful anguish)

Betrug! Betrug!	Tricked! Tricked! [4]
Schändlichster Betrug!	Shamefully tricked!
Verrat! Verrat!	Betrayed! Betrayed!
Wie noch nie er gerächt!	Like no one ever before!

GUTRUNE

Verrat? An wem?	Betrayed? How so?

ACT 2

[1] And here the orchestra insinuates the motif of the tarnhelmet that turned Siegfried into Gunther—and which currently dangles from Siegfried's belt:

Of course, Brünnhilde has known all along about the tarnhelmet from her father and, likewise, known that Siegfried now owns it. Small wonder she guesses what really happened.

[2] Flatly untrue. Siegfried took the ring from Brünnhilde only the night before—then described her capture in Scene 2, so his short-term memory is fully intact. But we've already heard him lie, and here he goes again: his denial is categorically false.

[3] Now he takes refuge in a half truth. Another step backward thanks to the dark elves?

[4] During these outbursts, p. 343 of the Dover full score (a facsimile of the 1877 Schott edition) asks the soprano to hold the notes until "she's almost out of breath."

ACT 2

CLANSMEN
Verrat? Verrat?
Betrayed? Betrayed?

WOMEN
Verrat? An wem?
Betrayed? How so?

BRÜNNHILDE
Heil'ge Götter,
himmlische Lenker!
Rauntet ihr dies
in eurem Rat?
Lehrt ihr mich Leiden,
wie keiner sie litt?
Schuft ihr mir Schmach,
wie nie sie geschmerzt?
Ratet nun Rache,
wie nie sie gerast!
Zündet mir Zorn,
wie noch nie er gezähmt!
Heißet Brünnhild,
ihr Herz zu zerbrechen,
den zu zertrümmern,
der sie betrog!

Gods on high,
heavenly governors!
You contrived this
in your conference?
You're giving me lessons
in unprecedented grief?
You're going to doom me
to unheard-of disgrace?
Then grant me vengeance
of unparalleled violence!
Goad me to anger
unmatched in this age! [1]
Ensure that Brünnhilde
breaks her heart in half
to bring down this man
who betrayed her!

GUNTHER
Brünnhild', Gemahlin!
Mäß'ge dich!
Brünnhilde, my bride!
Calm yourself!

BRÜNNHILDE
Weich' fern, Verräter!
Selbst verrat'ner!
Wisset denn Alle:
nicht ihm,
dem Manne dort
bin ich vermählt.

Stay away, villain!
Victim of self-deceit!
Hear me, all of you—
it isn't to him
but to that man there
that I'm married.

WOMEN
Siegfried? Gutrun's Gemahl?
Siegfried? Gutrune's spouse?

CLANSMEN
Gutrun's Gemahl?
Gutrune's spouse?

BRÜNNHILDE
Er zwang mir Lust
und Liebe ab.
He lured me to love
and pleasure him.

SIEGFRIED
Achtest du so
der eig'nen Ehre?
Have you no regard
for your reputation?

ACT 2

[1] She not only does her thinking with her heart, she has inherited Wotan's violent temper. The disillusionment and brutality she experienced the night before are making her easy prey for the dark elves.

ACT 2

Die Zunge, die sie lästert,	When your own tongue tarnishes it,
muß ich der Lüge sie zeihen?	must I accuse you of falsehood?
Hört, ob ich Treue brach!	Listen, and see if I broke faith!
Blutbrüderschaft	We're blood brothers,
hab ich Gunther geschworen.	I've bonded for life with Gunther.
Notung, das werte Schwert,	Notung, my noble weapon,
wahrte der Treue Eid:	witnessed how I kept my oath—
mich trennte seine Schärfe	I put its sharpness between us
von diesem traur'gen Weib.	to separate me from this hapless woman. [1]

BRÜNNHILDE

Du listiger Held,	You slippery hero,
sieh wie du lügst,	look how you lie,
wie auf dein Schwert	saying your sword
du schlecht dich berufst!	can vouch for your vow!
Wohl kenn ich seine Schärfe,	I'm familiar with its sharpness
doch kenn auch die Scheide,	and likewise with the sheath
darin so wonnig	hanging on the wall
ruht' an der Wand	that housed
Notung, der treue Freund,	Notung your faithful friend,
als die Traute sein Herr sich gewann.	while its master made love to his lady. [2]

(Clansmen huddle angrily with the women.)

CLANSMEN

Wie? Brach er die Treue?	What! He broke faith?
Trübte er Gunthers Ehre?	He blemished Gunther's honor?

WOMEN

Brach er die Treue?	He broke faith?

GUNTHER
(To Siegfried)

Geschändet wär' ich,	I'll live in disgrace,
schmählich bewahrt,	dishonored for life,
gäbst du die Rede	if you don't disprove
nicht ihr zurück!	what she says!

GUTRUNE

Treulos, Siegfried,	Siegfried, did
sannest du Trug?	you cheat on me?
Bezeuge, daß Jene	Speak the truth,
falsch dich zeiht!	challenge her testimony!

CLANSMEN

Reinige dich,	Salvage your reputation,
bist du im Recht!	if you're in the right!

ACT 2

[1] Poor bedeviled Siegfried finally thinks he's on firmer ground. No such luck.

[2] They first made love at the close of Day 2, and surely there were further occasions. Thanks to Hagen's potion, Siegfried remembers only the prior night when they abstained. Brünnhilde, of course, remembers the other nights.

ACT 2

Schweige die Klage! / Refute what she told us!
Schwöre den Eid! / Testify under oath!

SIEGFRIED

Schweig' ich die Klage, / I'll refute what she told us,
schwör' ich den Eid: / I'll testify under oath—
wer von euch wagt / who'll supply the weapon
seine Waffe daran? / on which I swear?

HAGEN

Meines Speeres Spitze / The point of my spear
wag ich daran: / will serve the purpose—
sie wahr' in Ehren den Eid! / and officially enforce your oath! [1]

*(The clansmen form a circle around Siegfried
and Hagen. The latter holds out his spear; Siegfried
lays two fingers of his right hand on its point.)*

SIEGFRIED

Helle Wehr, / Brilliant steel,
heilige Waffe: / blessed safeguard—
hilf meinem ewigen Eide! / enforce my oath for eternity!
Bei des Speeres Spitze / On your spearpoint
sprech ich den Eid: / I swear this oath—
Spitze, achte des Spruchs! / spearpoint, witness my words!
Wo Scharfes mich schneidet, / Where your sharpness can strike me,
schneide du mich; / strike away;
wo der Tod mich soll treffen, / where death must come to me,
treffe du mich: / let it come—
klagte das Weib dort wahr, / if this woman's accusation is accurate
brach ich dem Bruder den Eid. / and I broke my oath to my brother.

BRÜNNHILDE

*(Stepping furiously into the circle,
she snatches Siegfried's hand from the spear
and seizes its point with her own.)*

Helle Wehr, / Brilliant steel,
heilige Waffe: / blessed safeguard—
hilf meinem ewigen Eide! / enforce my oath for eternity!
Bei des Speeres Spitze / On your spearpoint
sprech ich den Eid: / I swear this oath—
Spitze, achte des Spruchs! / spearpoint, witness my words!
Ich weihe deine Wucht, / I sanctify your steel
daß sie ihn werfe! / so it can strike him!
Deine Schärfe segne ich, / I purify your point
daß sie ihn schneide! / so it can pierce him!
Denn, brach seine Eide er all, / Because, just as he broke his prior oaths,
schwur Meineid jetzt dieser Mann. / this man perjured himself once more.

ACT 2

[1] As he did in Act 1, it's Hagen who administers the oath; the dark elves have taken over Wotan's role. Once again, as Erda observes back in *Siegfried*, "everything on earth seems topsy-turvy!"

The god Donner in his heyday.
1882 ILLUSTRATION BY KARL EMIL DOEPLER

ACT 2

	CLANSMEN
	(In a total uproar)
Hilf, Donner!	Help, Donner!
Tose dein Wetter,	Call up a storm,
zu schweigen die wütende Schmach!	drown out this crying disgrace! [1]
	SIEGFRIED
Gunther, wehr deinem Weibe,	Gunther, look to your lady,
das schamlos Schande dir lügt!	her lies slander you shamelessly!
Gönnt ihr Weil' und Ruh',	Give her a moment to rest and relax,
der wilden Felsenfrau,	and the wild mountain woman
daß ihre freche Wut sich lege,	will stop these reckless ravings,
die eines Unholds	which some evil spirit
arge List	has slyly
wider uns Alle erregt!	roused against us all! [2]
Ihr Mannen, kehret euch ab,	So let's retreat and quit fighting
laßt das Weibergekeif!	with this quarrelsome female!
Als Zage weichen wir gern,	Clansmen, it's best to turn tail
gilt es mit Zungen den Streit.	when it comes to a battle of tongues.
	(Approaching Gunther)
Glaub', mehr zürnt es mich als dich,	Believe me, I'm bothered as well
daß schlecht ich sie getäuscht;	that I failed to fool her;
der Tarnhelm, dünkt mich fast,	the tarnhelmet, I suspect,
hat halb mich nur gehehlt.	didn't totally disguise me.
Doch Frauengroll	But ladies rarely
friedet sich bald;	rage for long;
daß ich dir es gewann,	She'll soon be grateful
dankt dir gewiß noch das Weib!	that I gained her for you!
	(Turning to the clansmen)
Munter, ihr Mannen!	Buck up, my lads!
Folgt mir zum Mahl!	Let's go to the banquet!
	(To the women)
Froh zur Hochzeit	We'd adore for you women
helfet, ihr Frauen!	to assist at the wedding!
Wonnige Lust	We'll fill your lives
lache nun auf!	with laughing and fun!
In Hof und Hain,	This court and countryside
heiter vor Allen,	will see that today
sollt ihr heute mich sehn.	I'm the cheeriest of all.
Wen die Minne freut,	So if you cherish
meinem frohen Mute	love and laughter,
tu es der Glückliche gleich!	join me and share in my joy!

ACT 2

[1] Donner's not about to answer, because the old regime is no more. The dark elves are in control now, and their governing style is starting to resemble anarchy.

[2] Even in his altered state Siegfried has an inkling of the truth. Unfortunately, he's too precoccupied to think things through.

ACT 2

*(In high good humor, Siegfried throws his arm around Gutrune
and takes her into the villa; encouraged by his example, women and clansmen
follow him. The stage empties out. Only Brünnhilde, Gunther, and Hagen remain behind.
Gunther sits down at one side and covers his face, deeply depressed and abjectly
ashamed. Watching in anguish as Siegfried and Gutrune disappear inside,
Brünnhilde remains standing downstage; she stares at the ground.)*

Scene 5

BRÜNNHILDE
(In a daze)

Welches Unholds List	What evil spirit
liegt hier verhohlen?	could spin such a plot?
Welches Zaubers Rat	What magic spells
regte dies auf?	made this possible? [1]
Wo ist nun mein Wissen	Why haven't I the wits
gegen dies Wirrsal?	to handle this situation?
Wo sind meine Runen	The runic wisdom
gegen dies Rätsel?	to solve this riddle?
Ach, Jammer! Jammer!	Oh horrible! Horrible!
Weh, ach Wehe!	What sorrow and pain!

(Breaking down)

All mein Wissen	All my understanding
wies ich ihm zu:	I've passed on to him—
in seiner Macht	it puts me utterly
hält er die Magd;	in his power;
in seinen Banden	now he takes
hält er die Beute,	this treasure
die, jammernd ob ihrer Schmach,	and, to my shame and sorrow,
jauchzend der Reiche verschenkt!	squanders it like a wealthy spendthrift!
Wer bietet mir nun das Schwert,	Where can I find the sword
mit dem ich die Bande zerschnitt'?	that will sever these fetters?

HAGEN
(Approaching Brünnhilde)

Vertraue mir, betrog'ne Frau!	Rely on me, afflicted woman!
Wer dich verriet,	I'll take revenge
das räche ich.	on your abuser.

BRÜNNHILDE
(Giving him a blank stare)

An wem?   On whom?

HAGEN

An Siegfried, der dich betrog.   On Siegfried, who betrayed you.

ACT 2

[1] Like Siegfried a page earlier, she also has an inkling of the truth. Alas, she too is in no state to sort things out.

ACT 2

An Siegfried? . . . du?

Ein einz'ger Blick
seines blitzenden Auges,
das selbst durch die Lügengestalt
leuchtend strahlte zu mir,
deinen besten Mut
machte er bangen.

Doch meinem Speere
spart ihn sein Meineid?

Eid, und Meineid—
müßige Acht!
Nach Stärk'rem späh,
deinen Speer zu waffnen,
willst du den Stärksten bestehn!

Wohl kenn ich Siegfrieds
siegende Kraft,
wie schwer im Kampf er zu fällen;
drum raune nun du
mir guten Rat,
e doch der Recke mir wich?

O, Undank! Schändlichster Lohn!
Nicht eine Kunst
war mir bekannt,
die zum Heil nicht half seinem Leib:
unwissend zähmt' ihn
mein Zauberspiel,
das ihn vor Wunden nun gewahrt.

So kann keine Wehr ihm schaden?

Im Kampfe nicht! Doch—
träfst du im Rücken ihn.
Niemals—das wußt ich—
wich' er dem Feind,
nie reicht' er fliehend ihm den Rücken:
an ihm drum spart' ich den Segen.

BRÜNNHILDE
On Siegfried . . . *you?*
(Caustically)
A single glance
from his flashing eyes,
whose gleam even his false disguise
couldn't conceal from my own, [1]
would cause your courage
to completely fail.

HAGEN
But shouldn't my spear
punish his perjury?

BRÜNNHILDE
Truth and perjury
are meaningless words!
You'll need stronger things
backing up your spear
to beat the mightiest of men!

HAGEN
I'm well aware of Siegfried's
awesome strength,
how difficult he is to defeat;
so could you give me
some good insights
into the warrior's weaknesses?

BRÜNNHILDE
Oh, how shamefully I'm repaid!
There isn't a blessing
I haven't provided
to shield his body and protect him always—
unbeknownst to him,
I cast a magic spell
that will make sure he stays uninjured.

HAGEN
So no weapon can wound him?

BRÜNNHILDE
Not in battle! Unless . . .
you took him from behind.
Never, I was positive,
would he turn tail and flee,
so I didn't protect his back from foes—
the spells I cast don't cover him there.

ACT 2

[1] See the stage directions describing her struggle with Siegfried at the end of Act 1.

Brünnhilde and Gunther.
ARTIST UNKNOWN; ILLUSTRATION IN BAKER'S
STORIES FROM NORTHERN MYTHS, 1914

ACT 2

HAGEN

Und dort trifft ihn mein Speer!	And there my spear will stab him!

(He instantly turns from Brünnhilde to Gunther)

Auf, Gunther!	Get up, Gunther!
Edler Gibichung!	Noble Gibichung!
Hier steht dein starkes Weib:	Here stands your stalwart wife—
was hängst du dort in Harm?	why are you hanging your head?

GUNTHER
(Bursting out in agony)

O Schmach!	I'm disgraced!
O Schande!	I'm dishonored!
Wehe mir,	Heaven help me,
dem jammervollsten Manne!	I'm the most dismal creature alive!

HAGEN

In Schande liegst du,	You're in disrepute,
leugn' ich das?	who can deny it?

BRÜNNHILDE
(To Gunther)

O feiger Mann!	You fraudulent coward!
Falscher Genoss'!	Counterfeit friend!
Hinter dem Helden	Hiding behind the hero
hehltest du dich,	and earning fame
daß Preise des Ruhmes	for feats he performed
er dir erränge!	in your place!
Tief wohl sank	Far indeed has
das teure Geschlecht,	your worthy race fallen
das solche Zagen gezeugt!	to father a weakling like you!

GUNTHER
(Utterly distraught)

Betrüger ich—und betrogen!	I'm a trickster . . . who was tricked!
Verräter ich—und verraten!	I'm a deceiver . . . who was deceived!
Zermalmt mir das Mark!	Break up my bones!
Zerbrecht mir die Brust!	Hack up my heart!
Hilf, Hagen!	Save me, Hagen!
Hilf meiner Ehre!	Save me from mortification!
Hilf deiner Mutter,	Save me for your mother's sake,
die mich auch ja gebar!	since she bore us both!

HAGEN

Dir hilft kein Hirn,	No agonizing
dir hilft keine Hand;	or actions will save you;
dir hilft nur—Siegfrieds Tod!	only one thing . . . Siegfried's death!

ACT 2

"And there my spear will stab him!"
1911 WATERCOLOR BY ARTHUR RACKHAM

ACT 2

GUNTHER
(Horrified)
Siegfried's death!

Siegfrieds Tod!

HAGEN
Only that will save you from shame!

Nur der sühnt deine Schmach!

GUNTHER
(Staring blankly)
We're blood brothers,
bound for life!

Blutbrüderschaft
schwuren wir uns!

HAGEN
For breaking your pact
he must pay with his blood!

Des Bundes Bruch
sühne nun Blut!

GUNTHER
He broke our pact?

Brach er den Bund?

HAGEN
And betrayed you.

Da er dich verriet.

GUNTHER
He betrayed me?

Verriet er mich?

BRÜNNHILDE
(Fiercely)
He betrayed you,
and I've been betrayed by you all!
If life were fair,
all the blood that flows
wouldn't cancel out your crimes!
But a single death
will satisfy me completely—
Siegfried must perish
to pay for your sins and his!

Dich verriet er,
und mich verrietet ihr Alle!
Wär' ich gerecht,
alles Blut der Welt
büßte mir nicht eure Schuld!
Doch des Einen Tod
taugt mir für Alle:
Siegfried falle
zur Sühne für sich und euch!

HAGEN
(Turning to Gunther)
He'll perish . . .
(Confidentially)
and you'll profit!
Tremendous power is yours
if you take the ring from him,
which his death will make possible.

Er falle

dir zum Heil!
Ungeheure Macht wird dir,
gewinnst von ihm du den Ring,
den der Tod ihm wohl nur entreißt.

ACT 2

1876 costume design for a youthful Gibichung by Carl Emil Doepler.

ACT 2

GUNTHER
(Hushed)
Brünnhilde's ring?

Brünnhildes Ring?

HAGEN
The Nibelung's band of gold!

Des Nibelungen Reif!

GUNTHER
(Letting out a sigh)
So this is the end of Siegfried!

So wär' es Siegfrieds Ende!

HAGEN
Everybody will benefit.

Uns Allen frommt sein Tod.

GUNTHER
But don't forget Gutrune,
whom I gave him to!
How could we ever face her,
if we executed her husband?

Doch Gutrune, ach,
der ich ihn gönnte!
Straften den Gatten wir so,
wie bestünden wir vor ihr?

BRÜNNHILDE
(Erupting furiously)
What good were my wits?
Or my runic wisdom?
In all of my anguish
I've only now realized—
it was Gutrune's sorcery
that stole my husband away! [1]
Long may she suffer!

Was riet mir mein Wissen?
Was wiesen mich Runen?
Im hilflosen Elend
achtet mir's hell:
Gutrune heißt der Zauber,
der den Gatten mir entzückt!
Angst treffe sie!

HAGEN
(To Gunther)
His death is likely to distress her,
so let's disguise the deed.
We'll take him hunting
tomorrow morning;
we'll give out he was brought down
by a savage boar that gored him.

Muß sein Tod sie betrüben,
verhehlt sei ihr die Tat.
Auf muntres Jagen
ziehen wir morgen;
der Edle braust uns voran—
ein Eber bracht ihn da um.

GUNTHER AND BRÜNNHILDE
That settles it!
Siegfried dies!
He'll pay for the shame
that he caused me!
He's trampled
our bonds of trust—

So soll es sein!
Siegfried falle!
Sühn' er die Schmach,
die er mir schuf!
Des Eides Treue
hat er getrogen:

ACT 2

[1] During rehearsals for the Cycle's 1876 premiere, its composer described Gutrune as possessing "enticing charms" (Porges, 135).

ACT 2

mit seinem Blut
büß er die Schuld!
Allrauner,
rächender Gott!
Schwurwissender
Eideshort!
Wotan!
Wende dich her!
Weise die schrecklich
heilige Schar,
hieher zu horchen
dem Racheschwur!

Sterb' er dahin,
der strahlende Held!
Mein ist der Hort,
mir muß er gehören.
Drum sei der Reif
ihm entrissen!
Albenvater,
gefallner Fürst!
Nachthüter!
Niblungenherr!
Alberich!
Achte auf mich!
Weise von neuem
der Niblungen Schar,
dir zu gehorchen,
des Reifes Herrn!

by giving his life
he'll purge his guilt!
All-knowing
god of revenge!
Truth-seeking
guardian of oaths!
Wotan!
Give ear to us!
Let your hallowed
hosts on high
listen to
this vow of vengeance!

HAGEN
He'll go to his grave,
the glorious hero!
The treasure's mine,
I'll be its master.
We'll get back
that band of gold!
Elf father,
fallen prince!
Protector of night!
Nibelung chief!
Alberich!
Hear my announcement!
Once more you'll bid
the Nibelung hosts
bow down to you
as ruler of the ring!

(As Gunther sweeps toward the villa with Brünnhilde, they meet the wedding party on its way out. Boys and girls prance merrily in front, waving wands adorned with flowers. Clansmen carry Siegfried on a shield, Gutrune on a chair. Coming down trails from the heights upstage, vassals and maidservants bear sacrificial beasts and equipment to the altar stones, which they deck with flowers. Siegfried and the clansmen blow their horns to summon the wedding guests. The women invite Brünnhilde to fall in beside Gutrune. Brünnhilde gives them a blank stare, then Gutrune beckons her with a friendly smile. Brünnhilde turns away sharply, but Hagen steps in at once and guides her to Gunther, who again takes her by the hand and then lets clansmen lift him onto a shield. Scarcely interrupted, the party moves briskly upstage as the curtain closes.) [1]

ACT 2

[1] Then the orchestra adds a grisly exclamation point, the macabre motif of Hagen's scheming:

ACT 2

LOOKING BACK ON ACT 2

Who's making it happen?
    1) Alberich indirectly.
    2) Hagen directly.

What's the plan?
    1) To get the ring, of course.
    2) Hagen knows it's with Brünnhilde.
    3) He jockeys Siegfried and Gunther into fetching her.

How's it working out?
    1) Ironically, Hagen is now administering oaths and serving as guardian of justice.
    2) Under the influence of mind-altering chemicals, Siegfried proves a poor schemer.
    3) In a state of shock, Brünnhilde goes on an emotional tear and is readily manipulated.
    4) When the ring arrives on site, Hagen takes advantage of events and improvises adroitly.
    5) To develop a justifiable claim to the ring, he recruits witnesses and public support.
    6) He takes sworn testimony from Siegfried, laying him open to perjury charges.
    7) If these charges can be proven, Siegfried will face the death penalty.
    8) Hagen's plan is to execute Siegfried in the field.
    9) Gunther and Brünnhilde are accessories before the fact.
    10) In Act 3 Hagen will hope to extract a public confession from Siegfried.

What else is upside down?
    1) Siegfried is in moral decline, planning deceptions, telling lies, committing cold-blooded violence.
    2) Brünnhilde exchanges adoring love for vehement hate—raging as one would expect of Wotan's daughter.

ACT 2

1876 costume design for a senior Gibichung by Carl Emil Doepler.

ACT 3

ACT 3

Prelude and Scene 1

*The curtain opens on the valley of the Rhine River,
which flows past a rugged, forest-covered bank upstage.
Woglinde, Wellgunde, and Flosshilde, the three Rhine daughters,
surface and swim in a circle as if dancing a roundelay.*

THE THREE RHINE DAUGHTERS
(Briefly interrupting their swimming)

Frau Sonne	Madame Sun
sendet lichte Strahlen;	sends her magnificent rays;
Nacht liegt in der Tiefe:	darkness lies in these depths—
einst war sie hell,	they once were lit up
da heil und hehr	when, safe and sacred,
des Vaters Gold noch in ihr glänzte.	father's gold still gleamed in them.
Rheingold!	Rhine Gold!
Klares Gold!	Radiant gold!
Wie hell du einsten strahltest,	Your streams of light would dazzle us,
hehrer Stern der Tiefe!	lordly star of the deep!

(They resume their aquatic roundelay.)

Weialala leia,	Weialala leia,
wallala leialala!	wallala leialala!

(There's a horn call in the distance. They listen, then splash around excitedly.)

Frau Sonne,	Madame Sun,
sende uns den Helden,	send us the hero
der das Gold uns wiedergebe!	who'll give us our gold once more!
Ließ' er es uns,	If we got back
dein lichtes Auge	its starry eye,
neideten dann wir nicht länger!	we'd stop being envious of you!
Rheingold!	Rhine Gold!
Klares Gold!	Radiant gold!
Wie froh du dann strahltest,	Your sovereign light would dazzle again,
freier Stern der Tiefe!	liberated star of the deep!

(Siegfried's horn rings out nearer to hand.)

WOGLINDE

Ich höre sein Horn.	I hear his horn call.

WELLGUNDE

Der Helde naht.	The hero's close by.

FLOSSHILDE

Laßt uns beraten!	Let's put our heads together!

ACT 3

Design sketch by Josef Hoffmann: Act 3 of *Twilight for the Gods* at its 1876 Bayreuth premiere.

ACT 3

*(All three instantly dive below. In hunting regalia,
Siegfried steps out onto an overhanging bank.)*

SIEGFRIED

Ein Albe führte mich irr,	Some elf led me astray,
daß ich die Fährte verlor.	and I've lost my way. [1]
He, Schelm! In welchem Berge	Hey, you scamp! Where in these hills
bargst du so schnell mir das Wild?	have you suddenly hidden the game?

THE THREE RHINE DAUGHTERS
(Surfacing again and returning to their roundelay)

Siegfried!   Siegfried!

FLOSSHILDE

Was schiltst du so in den Grund?   Why are you so grumpy?

WELLGUNDE

Welchem Alben bist du gram?   What elf is giving you trouble?

WOGLINDE

Hat dich ein Nicker geneckt?   Is some sprite teasing you?

THE THREE RHINE DAUGHTERS

Sag es, Siegfried, sag es uns!   Tell us, Siegfried, tell us about it!

SIEGFRIED
(Grinning at them)

Entzückt ihr euch zu euch	Did you share yourselves
den zottigen Gesellen,	with that shaggy varmint
der mir verschwand?	who just vanished?
Ist's euer Friedel,	If he's a lover of yours,
euch lustigen Frauen	you lighthearted women
laß ich ihn gern!	are welcome to him!

(The girls laugh.)

WOGLINDE

Siegfried, was gibst du uns,	Siegfried, what'll you give us
wenn wir das Wild dir gönnen?	if we get you some game?

SIEGFRIED

Noch bin ich beutelos;	I've had no luck as yet;
so bittet, was ihr begehrt!	so say what you're looking for!

WELLGUNDE

Ein gold'ner Ring	A golden ring is
glänzt dir am Finger:	gleaming on your finger—

ACT 3

[1] He has another inkling of the truth. This sentence sums up his entire situation.

Siegfried and the Rhine daughters.
FROM AN 1891 PAINTING BY ALBERT PINKHAM RYDER

ACT 3

THE THREE RHINE DAUGHTERS

Den gib uns!   Give us that!

SIEGFRIED

Einen Riesenwurm / I conquered a dragon
erschlug ich um den Reif, / to capture this ring,
für eines schlechten Bären Tatzen / and you'd like me to barter it
böt' ich ihn nun zum Tausch? / for some lowly bearskin?

WOGLINDE

Bist du so karg?   Are you so cheap?

WELLGUNDE

So geizig beim Kauf?   So chintzy in your dealings?

FLOSSHILDE

Freigebig / Be charitable
solltest Frauen du sein. / with the ladies in your life.

SIEGFRIED

Verzehrt' ich an euch mein Gut, / If I waste my wealth on you women,
des zürnte mir wohl mein Weib. / my wife will be perturbed with me.

FLOSSHILDE

Sie ist wohl schlimm?   Does she pick on you?

WELLGUNDE

Sie schlägt dich wohl?   Does she punish you?

WOGLINDE

Ihre Hand fühlt schon der Held!   I bet he's felt the back of her hand!

(They laugh raucously.)

SIEGFRIED

Nun lacht nur lustig zu! / Go and laugh all you like!
In Harm laß ich euch doch: / You aren't getting your way—
denn giert ihr nach dem Ring, / however much you want this ring,
euch Nickern geb ich ihn nie! / I won't let you water sprites have it!

(The Rhine daughters continue their roundelay.)

FLOSSHILDE

So schön!   So handsome!

WELLGUNDE

So stark!   So husky!

ACT 3

"Be charitable with the ladies in your life."
1896 PAINTING BY FERDINAND LEEKE

ACT 3

WOGLINDE

So gehrenswert!	So huggable!

THE THREE RHINE DAUGHTERS

Wie schade, daß er geizig ist!	It's a pity he's a penny-pincher!

(They laugh and dive below.)

SIEGFRIED
(Descending the riverbank)

Was leid ich doch	Why should I tolerate
das karge Lob?	their teasing?
Laß ich so mich schmähn?	Why let them laugh at me?
Kämen sie wieder	If these women return
zum Wasserrand,	to the water's edge,
den Ring könnten sie haben.	they can have the ring.

(Calling to them)

He! Hehe! Ihr munt'ren	Hey! Hey there! You carefree
Wasserminnen!	river creatures!
Kommt rasch! Ich schenk euch den Ring!	Hurry back! I'll hand the ring to you!

(He slips the ring off his finger and holds it in the air. The Rhine daughters return to the surface. Their faces are solemn and serious.)

FLOSSHILDE

Behalt ihn, Held,	Hold on to it, hero,
und wahr ihn wohl,	and look after it
bis du das Unheil errätst,	till you learn of the evil . . .

WOGLINDE AND WELLGUNDE

das in dem Ring du hegst.	. . . lying in that ring of yours.

THE THREE RHINE DAUGHTERS

Froh fühlst du dich dann	Then you'll feel so grateful
befrei'n wir dich von dem Fluch.	we freed you from the curse's grip.

SIEGFRIED
(Quietly putting the ring back on his finger)

So singet, was ihr wißt.	Sing away, speak your piece. [1]

THE THREE RHINE DAUGHTERS

Siegfried! Siegfried! Siegfried!	Siegfried! Siegfried! Siegfried!
Schlimmes wissen wir dir.	We see perils in store for you.

WELLGUNDE

Zu deinem Unheil	You'll come to grief
wahrst du den Ring!	unless you give up the ring!

ACT 3

[1] The daughters display this behavior pattern back in the Cycle's opening scene: after flirting with Alberich, they turn grimly serious to describe the ring. Both then and now they manufacture trouble for themselves— why do such a risky thing?

Prior to Alberich and Siegfried, could such warnings of sacrifice and disaster have successfully discouraged would-be thieves?

ACT 3

THE THREE RHINE DAUGHTERS

Aus des Rheines Gold	From the river's pure gold
ist der Ring geglüht:	that ring was annealed— [1]

WELLGUNDE

der ihn listig geschmiedet,   he who adroitly shaped it . . .

WOGLINDE

und schmählich verlor,   . . . and lost it to his shame . . .

THE THREE RHINE DAUGHTERS

der verfluchte ihn,	. . . laid a curse on it
in fernster Zeit,	to last for eternity,
zu zeugen den Tod	promising death
dem, der ihn trüg.	to people who wear it.

FLOSSHILDE

Wie den Wurm du fälltest,   Just as the dragon perished,

WELLGUNDE AND FLOSSHILDE

so fällst auch du,   . . . you'll perish as well . . .

THE THREE RHINE DAUGHTERS

und heute noch:	. . . this very day—
so heißen wir's dir,	that's what we predict,
tauschest den Ring du uns nicht,	if you don't return the ring to us,

WELLGUNDE AND FLOSSHILDE.

im tiefen Rhein ihn zu Bergen.   . . . to its depository deep in the Rhine.

THE THREE RHINE DAUGHTERS

Nur seine Flut	Only its waters
sühnet den Fluch!	can wash away the curse!

SIEGFRIED

Ihr listigen Frauen,	You cunning hussies,
laßt das sein!	I've heard enough!
Traut' ich kaum eurem Schmeicheln,	I didn't think much of your flattery,
euer Drohen schreckt mich noch minder!	and your threats don't frighten me either!

THE THREE RHINE DAUGHTERS

Siegfried! Siegfried!	Siegfried! Siegfried!
Wir weisen dich wahr:	We're telling the truth—
weiche, weiche dem Fluch!	capitulate, escape the curse!
Ihn flochten nächtlich	Working in the night,
webende Nornen	the Norns wove it
in des Urgesetzes Seil!	into the thread of destiny!

ACT 3

[1] Heat treatment in metalworking that makes the substance more malleable.

Doomsaying Rhine daughters.
IN A VICTORIAN LITHOGRAPH BY
HENRI FANTIN-LATOUR

ACT 3

SIEGFRIED

Mein Schwert zerschwang einen Speer:	My sword once sliced a spear in half— [1]
des Urgesetzes	so it'll be with
ewiges Seil,	the thread of destiny
flochten sie wilde	and any threatening
Flüche hinein,	curses it contains—
Notung zerhaut es den Nornen!	Notung will hack it from the Norns' hands!
Wohl warnte mich einst	In days gone by a dragon
vor dem Fluch ein Wurm,	told me about the curse,
doch das Fürchten lehrt er mich nicht.	though he didn't teach me to fear.

(He studies the ring.)

Der Welt Erbe	The earth's riches
gewänne mir ein Ring:	could be mine with this ring—
für der Minne Gunst	but for the pleasures of love
miß ich ihn gern,	I'd easily let it go
ich geb ihn euch, gönnt ihr mir Gunst.	and pay it to earn your affection.
Doch, bedroht ihr mir Leben und Leib,	But by threatening life and limb,
faßte er nicht	even if the thing
eines Fingers Wert,	were worth little,
den Reif entringt ihr mir nicht.	you'll never get this ring from me.
Denn Leben und Leib,	As for my own life and limbs,
seht:	look—

(He grabs a clump of dirt, holds it up, and tosses it over his shoulder.)

so—	to me,
werf ich sie weit von mir!	that's how much they mean! [2]

THE THREE RHINE DAUGHTERS

Kommt, Schwestern!	Let's go, sisters!
Schwindet dem Toren!	Say good-bye to this lunatic!
So weise und stark	As brilliant and powerful
verwähnt sich der Held,	as he thinks he is,
als gebunden und blind er doch ist!	he's a puppet and thoroughly blind! [3]

(They approach him, then noisily swim around in wider and wider circles.)

Eide schwur er,	He's oblivious
und achtet sie nicht!	to his oaths!

(Piling it on)

Runen weiß er,	He can't remember
und rät sie nicht!	his runic lessons!

FLOSSHILDE, THEN WOGLINDE.

Ein hehrstes Gut	He was granted
ward ihm gegönnt:	an incomparable gift—

[1] His memories of disarming Wotan are intact.

[2] The Wanderer's words still hold good: "Everything remains true to itself." Like Brünnhilde late in Act 1, Siegfried is also staying in character—he's the youth who hasn't learned to fear.

[3] It's hard to argue with this assessment. Unlike Brünnhilde and the man himself, the sprites know that Siegfried's memory has been tampered with.

ACT 3

THE THREE RHINE DAUGHTERS

daß er's verworfen,	. . . which he's gotten rid of
weiß er nicht;	and doesn't realize;

FLOSSHILDE

nur den Ring,   thanks to the ring . . .

WELLGUNDE

der zum Tod ihm taugt—   . . . he's under threat of death . . .

THE THREE RHINE DAUGHTERS

den Reif nur will er sich wahren!	. . . due to that band of gold he won't give up!
Leb wohl, Siegfried!	Good-bye, Siegfried!
Ein stolzes Weib	A valiant lady
wird noch heut dich Argen beerben:	will soon possess your property—
sie beut uns bess'res Gehör.	we'll visit her, and she'll listen to us. [1]
Zu ihr! Zu ihr! Zu ihr!	To her! To her! To her!

(They instantly turn, resume their roundelay, and swim upstage. Siegfried grins and watches them, his foot on a ledge, chin in his hand.)

Weialala leia,	Weialala leia,
Wallala leialala!	Wallala leialala!

SIEGFRIED

Im Wasser wie am Lande	In the water or on dry land,
lernte nun ich Weiber Art:	I've learned what women do—
wer nicht ihrem Schmeicheln traut,	they hold you in thrall with flattery
den schrecken sie mit Drohen;	or frighten you with threats;
wer dem nun kühnlich trotzt,	and if you talk back to a lady,
dem kommt dann ihr Keifen dran!	brace yourself for a tongue-lashing!

(The Rhine daughters are completely out of sight.)

Und doch,	And yet,
trüg' ich nicht Gutrun' Treu,	if I weren't Gutrune's spouse,
der zieren Frauen eine	one of those attractive girls
hätt' ich mir—frisch gezähmt!	would soon . . . be in my arms!

(The Rhine daughters are faintly audible in the distance. He gazes after them. Hunting horns ring out nearer and nearer from the rugged bank upstage.)

HAGEN'S VOICE
(Far off)

Hoiho!

(Siegfried snaps out of his ruminations and answers the horn calls with his own.)

ACT 3

[1] They mean Brünnhilde, as we'll see.

"To her! To her! To her!"
FROM A 1911 WATERCOLOR
BY ARTHUR RACKHAM

ACT 3

Scene 2

CLANSMEN
(Offstage)

Hoiho! Hoiho!   Hoiho! Hoiho!

SIEGFRIED
(Replying)

Hoiho! Hoiho! Hoihe!   Hoiho! Hoiho! Hoihe!

(Hagen appears on the bank with Gunther behind him.)

HAGEN
(Seeing Siegfried)

Finden wir endlich	So we've finally found
wohin du flogest?	where you went off to?

SIEGFRIED

Kommt herab! Hier ist frisch und kühl!	Come on down! It's cool and comfortable!

(The clansmen all appear on the bank and descend with Hagen and Gunther.)

HAGEN

Hier rasten wir,	Rest a while, men,
und rüsten das Mahl!	and get a meal ready!

(They bring over the day's haul.)

Laßt ruhn die Beute,	Put the game in a pile
und bietet die Schläuche!	and pass the wineskins!

(Wineskins and drinking horns materialize. Everybody relaxes.)

Der uns das Wild verscheuchte,	Now that he's scared off the wildlife,
nun sollt ihr Wunder hören,	let's hear from Siegfried about
was Siegfried sich erjagt.	his wondrous hunting.

SIEGFRIED

Schlimm steht es um mein Mahl:	I haven't a crumb to contribute—
von eurer Beute	I'll have to beg
bitte ich für mich.	a few bites from you.

HAGEN

Du beutelos?	You caught nothing?

SIEGFRIED

Auf Waldjagd zog ich aus,	I was after woodland critters,
doch Wasserwild zeigte sich nur:	but only water dwellers appeared—
war ich dazu recht beraten,	yet I didn't catch what turned up,

ACT 3

1876 costume designs for Gibichung huntsmen by Carl Emil Doepler.

ACT 3

drei wilde Wasservögel	a trio of wild waterfowl
hätt' ich euch wohl gefangen,	that shouldn't have evaded me,
die dort auf dem Rhein mir sangen,	but by the Rhine they serenaded me
erschlagen würd ich noch heut.	and said that I'd be slain today.

(Gunther winces, then frowns at Hagen. Siegfried sits down between them.)

HAGEN

Das wäre üble Jagd,	What bad luck it would be
wenn den Beutelosen selbst	if the hunter didn't bag a thing
ein lauernd Wild erlegte.	and got harmed by a lurking beast.

SIEGFRIED

Mich dürstet!	I'm thirsty. [1]

HAGEN
(Signaling for a filled drinking horn and handing it to him)

Ich hörte sagen, Siegfried,	Legend has it, Siegfried,
der Vögel Sangessprache	that birds speak a language
verstündest du wohl:	you can understand—
so wäre das wahr?	any truth to that?

SIEGFRIED

Seit lange acht ich	It's been a long time since
des Lallens nicht mehr.	I've listened to their twittering. [2]

(He lifts the drinking horn, takes a swig, then turns and offers it to Gunther.)

Trink, Gunther, trink:	Drink, Gunther, drink—
dein Bruder bringt es dir!	try your brother's brew!

(Gunther looks gloomily into the horn.)

GUNTHER
(Uneasily)

Du mischtest matt und bleich:	The mixture's bland and pale—

(His voice sinking still more)

dein Blut allein darin!	only *your* blood is in it!

SIEGFRIED
(Laughing)

So misch es mit dem deinen!	Then mix in some of yours!

(He tops it off with wine from Gunther's horn; it overflows.)

Nun floß gemischt es über:	The mixture's spilling over—
der Mutter Erde	so Mother Earth
laß das ein Labsal sein!	can also enjoy a sip!

ACT 3

[1] For knowledge? The truth? To learn what in blazes is going on?

[2] In the past such voices of Nature had alerted him to Mime's murder scheme. Now he's facing the same threat from Hagen & Co. but without his earlier guidance.

Siegfried has never been more alone.

ACT 3

GUNTHER
(Heaving a sigh)

Du überfroher Held!	You overexuberant man! [1]

SIEGFRIED
(Quietly to Hagen)

Ihm macht Brünnhilde Müh?	Is he brooding about Brünnhilde?

HAGEN
(Answering quietly)

Verstünd' er sie so gut,	He isn't sensitive to women
wie du der Vögel Sang!	the way you are to songbirds!

SIEGFRIED

Seit Frauen ich singen hörte,	Since I've heard ladies warble,
vergaß ich der Vöglein ganz.	I've lost interest in wildfowl. [2]

HAGEN

Doch einst vernahmst du sie?	But you understood them in the past?

SIEGFRIED
(Turning impulsively to Gunther)

Hei! Gunther,	Hey, Gunther,
grämlicher Mann!	you're so gloomy!
Dankst du es mir,	If it'll cheer you up,
so sing ich dir Mären	I'll tell you some tales
aus meinen jungen Tagen.	from my childhood.

GUNTHER

Die hör ich gern.	I'm happy to hear them.

(Everybody stretches out nearby or downstage of Siegfried, who's the only one sitting upright.)

HAGEN

So singe, Held!	Sing to us, hero!

SIEGFRIED

Mime hieß	Mime was
ein mürrischer Zwerg;	a disgruntled dwarf;
in des Neides Zwang	eaten by envy,
zog er mich auf,	he brought me up,
daß einst das Kind,	so when the boy
wann kühn es erwuchs,	grew big and brave,
einen Wurm ihm fällt im Wald,	he'd defeat a dragon in the woods,
der lang schon hütet einen Hort.	where it long had guarded a pile of gold.
Er lehrte mich schmieden	He taught me to be a smith
und Erze schmelzen;	and how to smelt ore;

ACT 3

[1] Siegfried in a nutshell.

[2] In other words, he's become a skirt chaser, a social butterfly, and deaf to the natural voices within him.

doch, was der Künstler
selber nicht konnt',
des Lehrlings Mute
mußt' es gelingen:
eines zerschlag'nen Stahles Stücken
neu zu schweißen zum Schwert.
Des Vaters Wehr
fügt' ich mir neu,
nagelfest
schuf ich mir Notung.
Tüchtig zum Kampf
dünkt' er dem Zwerg;
der führte mich nun zum Wald:
dort fällt' ich Fafner, den Wurm.
Jetzt aber merkt
wohl auf die Mär:
Wunder muß ich euch melden.
Von des Wurmes Blut
mir brannten die Finger,
sie führt' ich kühlend zum Mund:
kaum netzt' ein wenig
die Zunge das Naß,
was da die Vöglein sangen,
das konnt' ich flugs verstehn.
Auf den Ästen saß es und sang:
»Hei! Siegfried gehört nun
der Niblungen Hort!
O, fänd' in der Höhle
den Hort er jetzt!
Wollt' er den Tarnhelm gewinnen,
der taugt' ihm zu wonniger Tat:
doch wollt' er den Ring sich gewinnen,
der macht' ihn zum Walter der Welt!«

Ring und Tarnhelm
trugst du nun fort?

Das Vöglein hörtest du wieder?

Ring und Tarnhelm
hatt' ich gerafft:
da lauscht' ich wieder
dem wonnigen Laller;
der saß im Wipfel und sang:
»Hei! Siegfried gehört nun

ACT 3

but a deed that the craftsman
couldn't carry off himself
his daring apprentice
was due to accomplish—
there were some bits of broken blade
I had to weld again into a weapon.
My father's sword
took form again,
tough as nails
like Notung was before.
The dwarf figured
I was ready to fight;
he led me into the forest—
there I defeated Fafner the dragon.
However, note well
what happened next—
now I'll mention a marvelous thing.
The dragon's blood
burned my fingers,
which I stuck in my mouth to soothe—
my tongue no sooner
had touched the blood
than I heard the birds singing
and understood what they said.
Sitting on a limb, one of them sang—
"Hey, Siegfried can now take
the Nibelung's treasure!
He'll find it in the cave
where it's concealed!
If he fetches the tarnhelmet,
it will help him work marvels—
but if he wears the ring on his hand,
it will make him ruler of the world!"

HAGEN
You took the ring
and the tarnhelmet?

A CLANSMAN
Did you hear from the bird again?

SIEGFRIED
I retrieved the helmet
and the ring—
then I listened again
to the lovely warbler,
who sat in the treetop and sang—
"Hey, Siegfried now has

ACT 3

Siegfried stands to look at the ravens.
1911 WATERCOLOR BY ARTHUR RACKHAM

ACT 3

der Helm und der Ring!	the helmet and ring!
O traute er Mime	But he mustn't trust
dem treulosen nicht!	treacherous Mime!
Ihm sollt' er den Hort nur erheben;	The dwarf's trying to seize the treasure; [1]
nun lauert er listig am Weg;	he's lurking there, lying in wait—
nach dem Leben trachtet er Siegfried:	he wants to take Siegfried's life . . .
O, traute Siegfried nicht Mime!«	oh, Siegfried mustn't trust Mime!"

HAGEN

Er mahnte dich gut?   Was that precious advice?

FOUR CLANSMEN

Vergaltest du Mime?   You paid Mime back?

SIEGFRIED

Mit tödlichem Tranke	Carrying a deadly drink,
trat er zu mir;	he came up to me;
bang und stotternd	his mumbling and shaking
gestand er mir Böses:	showed his malicious intent—
Notung streckte den Strolch!	Notung laid him low!

HAGEN
(Letting out a guffaw)

Was nicht er geschmiedet	Mime couldn't fix it,
schmeckte doch Mime!	but it sure fixed him!

(He takes a new drinking horn and squeezes some drops from a medicinal plant into it.)

TWO CLANSMEN
(One after the other)

Was wies das Vöglein dich wieder?   Did the bird speak to you again?

HAGEN

Trink' erst, Held,	First, hero, have a sip
aus meinem Horn:	from my drinking horn—
ich würzte dir holden Trank,	I've flavored it with an ingredient
die Erinnerung hell dir zu wecken,	that will freshen your recollection, [2]

(He hands the horn to Siegfried.)

daß Fernes nicht dir entfalle!   so you recall your past perfectly!

SIEGFRIED
(Staring pensively into the horn, then slowly drinking)

In Leid zu dem Wipfel	I sadly looked up
lauscht' ich hinauf;	and listened;
da saß es noch und sang:	it still sat there and sang:
»Hei! Siegfried erschlug nun	"Hey, Siegfried has now slain
den schlimmen Zwerg!	the sinister dwarf!

ACT 3

[1] Here Siegfried changes the Woodbird's lyrics, presumably to clarify the storyline for his audience's benefit.

[2] In other words, an antidote to the original.

ACT 3

Jetzt wüßt' ich ihm noch das herrlichste Weib: auf hohem Felsen sie schläft, Feuer umbrennt ihren Saal: durchschritt' er die Brunst, weckt' er die Braut, Brünnhilde wäre dann sein!«	It so happens I've heard of a marvelous maiden for him— she's sleeping on a mountaintop, fire surrounds the spot— if he went though the blaze and woke up the woman, Brünnhilde would be his bride!"

HAGEN

Und folgtest du des Vögleins Rate?	And did you do what the bird directed?

SIEGFRIED

Rasch ohne Zögern zog ich nun aus:	I set out for the spot as swiftly as I could—

(Gunther listens with growing surprise.)

bis den feurigen Fels ich traf; die Lohe durchschritt ich, und fand zum Lohn—	I made it to the fiery mountain; I raced through the flames and was rewarded by finding . . .

(With increasing rapture)

schlafend ein wonniges Weib in lichter Waffen Gewand. Den Helm löst' ich der herrlichen Maid; mein Kuß erweckte sie kühn: oh! wie mich brünstig da umschlang der schönen Brünnhilde Arm!	. . . a wondrous woman who slept in a suit of shining armor. I removed the helmet from the heavenly maiden. I had the bravery to kiss her awake— oh, how ardently the beautiful Brünnhilde took me in her arms!

GUNTHER
(On his feet in absolute shock)

Was hör ich?	What am I hearing?

(Two ravens dart from a bush, circle above Siegfried, then fly off toward the Rhine.) [1]

HAGEN
(To Siegfried)

Errätst du auch dieser Raben Geraun?	Could you also sense what those ravens just said?

(Siegfried stands to look at the ravens, turning his back on Hagen.)

Rache rieten sie mir!	Take revenge, they told me!

*(Hagen drives his spear into Siegfried's back.
Gunther and the clansmen fling themselves on Hagen. [2]
Siegfried lifts his shield with both hands and swings it around to
smash down on Hagen; his strength gives out, the shield
drops behind him, and he falls backward onto it.)*

ACT 3

[1] Waltraute told us about them in Act 1: while somberly waiting in Valhalla, Wotan "sent out his two ravens to see what's transpiring."

[2] Too late, Gunther realizes what his sister will soon realize as well: Siegfried was Hagen's innocent victim, and "Brünnhilde was his dearly beloved, whom the drink made him forget!"

ACT 3

FOUR CLANSMEN
(Unable to stop Hagen)

Hagen, was tust du?	Hagen, what are you doing?

TWO OTHER CLANSMEN

Was tatest du?	What have you done?

GUNTHER

Hagen, was tatest du?	Hagen . . . what have you done?

HAGEN

Meineid rächt' ich!	Punished his perjury! [1]

(Hagen coolly turns and proceeds up the bank, still visible as he slowly walks into the twilight that's been descending since the ravens flew off. Grief-stricken, Gunther is at Siegfried's side and bending over him. The clansmen gather compassionately around the dying man.)

SIEGFRIED
(Sitting up and supported by two clansmen, his eyes wide open and glistening)

Brünnhilde!	Brünnhilde!
Heilige Braut!	Heavenly bride!
Wach auf! Öffne dein Auge!	Wake up! Open your eyes!
Wer verschloß dich	Who sealed you
wieder in Schlaf?	in slumber again?
Wer band dich in Schlummer so bang?	Who bound you in sleep's fearful bonds?
Der Wecker kam;	Your awakener is here;
er küßt dich wach;	you'll arise at his kiss;
und aber—der Braut	and again . . . the bride
bricht er die Bande:	will break free of her bonds—
da lacht ihm Brünnhildes Lust.	then he'll bask in Brünnhilde's joy.
Ach! Dieses Auge	Ah, these eyes
ewig nun offen!	now are open forever!
Ach, dieses Atems	Ah, this breathing
wonniges Wehen!	exhales enchantment!
Süßes Vergehen,	Happy departure,
seliges Grauen!	heavenly dawning!
Brünnhild' bietet mir—Gruß!	Brünnhilde bids me . . . hello!

(He sinks back and dies. Those around him are motionless with grief. [2] Night has fallen. Gunther silently signals the clansmen to lift Siegfried's body; they carry it slowly and solemnly up the bank. The moon breaks through the clouds and shines with increasing radiance on the funeral procession, now at the top of the river valley. Mists rise from the Rhine, gradually fill the entire stage, and leave the funeral party invisible during the orchestral interlude that follows; then the mists part and reveal the Gibichung villa as it looked in Act 1.)

ACT 3

[1] The payoff for Hagen's adroit improvising. He has administered both oaths sworn by Siegfried: a) the blood-brother pact in Act 1 (where Siegfried demands his own death "if he's false to his friend") and b) the sworn testimony in Act 2 (where Siegfried invites Hagen's spear to "strike me [if] I broke my oath to my brother"). The two oaths reinforce each other.

Accordingly, Hagen jockeys Siegfried into a public confession, executes him, and hopes the clansmen will view the execution as lawful and warranted. Hagen has taken over Wotan's role but subverted the god's ideals.

[2] What's most poignant about the death of this dazzling young man is his perishing in complete ignorance and innocence. He never gets a chance to understand.

Scene 3

(It's night. The Rhine reflects the rays of the moon. Gutrune comes out of her room in the villa.)

GUTRUNE

War das sein Horn? / Was that his horn call?

(Listening)

Nein! Noch
kehrt er nicht heim.
Schlimme Träume
störten mir den Schlaf.
Wild wieherte sein Roß;
Lachen Brünnhildes
weckte mich auf.
Wer war das Weib,
das ich zum Ufer schreiten sah?
Ich fürchte Brünnhild.
Ist sie daheim?

No! He still
isn't home yet.
Terrible dreams
kept troubling my sleep.
His horse neighed so noisily;
Brünnhilde laughed
and woke me. [1]
Was she the woman
I saw walking down to the river?
Brünnhilde scares me.
Is she in her room?

(She listens at the door audience right and calls out.)

Brünnhild'! Brünnhild'!
Bist du wach?

Brünnhilde! Brünnhilde!
Are you up?

(She opens it gingerly and looks into the room.)

Leer das Gemach.
So war es sie,
die ich zum Rheine schreiten sah?
War das sein Horn?
Nein!
Öd alles!

Her room's empty.
So it was she
I saw walking down to the Rhine?
Was that his horn call?
No!
Nobody's here!

(She looks anxiously outside.)

Säh ich Siegfried nur bald! / I hope Siegfried is home soon!

(She hears Hagen's voice and stands still for a moment, seized with fear.)

HAGEN'S VOICE
(Outside and coming nearer)

Hoiho! Hoiho!
Wacht auf! Wacht auf!
Lichte! Lichte,
helle Brände!
Jagdbeute
bringen wir heim.
Hoiho! Hoiho!

Hoiho! Hoiho!
Wake up! Wake up!
Fetch torches,
flaming firebrands!
We're bringing home
booty from the hunt.
Hoiho! Hoiho!

(Lights outside come nearer. Hagen enters the villa.)

ACT 3

[1] What on earth could Brünnhilde have to laugh about? We'll speculate later.

The funeral party bearing Siegfried's body.
ENGRAVING OF AN 1889 GOUACHE PAINTING BY HOWARD PYLE

ACT 3

Auf, Gutrun'!
Begrüße Siegfried!
Der starke Held,
er kehret heim.

Come, Gutrune!
Greet Siegfried!
The stalwart hero
is hurrying home.

GUTRUNE
(Seriously alarmed)

Was geschah? Hagen!
Nicht hört' ich sein Horn!

What happened, Hagen?
I didn't hear his horn call!

(Huge hubbub. Women and clansmen with torches enter beside the funeral party bearing Siegfried's body.)

HAGEN

Der bleiche Held,
nicht bläst er es mehr;
nicht stürmt er zur Jagd,
zum Streite nicht mehr,
noch wirbt er um wonnige Frauen!

The pale hero
will play no more tunes;
nor dash off again
to duels or the hunt,
or to court some comely maiden!

GUTRUNE
(In growing fear)

Was bringen die?

What are they bearing?

(Now inside the villa, clansmen set the body down on a hastily improvised bier.)

HAGEN.

Eines wilden Ebers Beute:
Siegfried, deinen toten Mann!

A vicious boar's victim—
Siegfried, your slain husband!

(Gutrune shrieks and collapses. Gunther comforts her. All react with shock and grief.)

GUNTHER

Gutrun', holde Schwester!
Hebe dein Auge,
schweige mir nicht!

Gutrune, sweet sister!
Open your eyes,
say something!

GUTRUNE
(Coming to, then pushing Gunther away)

Siegfried—Siegfried—erschlagen!
Fort, treuloser Bruder,
du Mörder meines Mannes!
O Hilfe! Hilfe!
Wehe! Wehe!
Sie haben Siegfried erschlagen!

Siegfried . . . Siegfried . . . slain!
Get away, malicious brother,
murderer of my husband!
Oh help! Help!
Horror and misery!
They've slaughtered Siegfried!

GUNTHER

Nicht klage wider mich!
Dort klage wider Hagen:

I didn't commit the crime!
It's Hagen who's the culprit—

ACT 3

"It was she I saw walking down to the Rhine?"
1914 ILLUSTRATION BY FRANZ STASSEN

ACT 3

er ist der verfluchte Eber,
der diesen Edlen zerfleischt.

                he's the cursed boar
                who cut the hero down.

HAGEN

Bist du mir gram darum?
                So you blame me now?

GUNTHER

Angst und Unheil
greife dich immer!
                May fear and dread
                dog you forever!

HAGEN
(Confronting them, fiercely defiant)

Ja denn! Ich hab
ihn erschlagen.
Ich—Hagen—
schlug ihn zu Tod.
Meinem Speer war er gespart,
bei dem er Meineid sprach.
Heiliges Beuterecht
hab ich mir nun errungen:
d'rum fordr' ich hier diesen Ring.
                Yes, it was I, Hagen,
                whose weapon slew him.
                I ran it through him
                and put him to death.
                My spear had to enforce the oath
                he soiled with his perjury.
                By right of conquest
                this is my sacred payment—
                I claim his ring as my reward.

GUNTHER

Zurück! Was mir verfiel,
sollst nimmer du empfahn!
                It's mine, hands off,
                don't you dare lay hold of it!

HAGEN

Ihr Mannen, richtet mein Recht!
                Clansmen, support my claim! [1]

GUNTHER

Rührst du an Gutrunes Erbe,
schamloser Albensohn?
                Will you steal Gutrune's heritage,
                you shameless son of an elf?

HAGEN
(Drawing his sword) [2]

Des Alben Erbe
fordert so sein Sohn!
                The elf's heritage
                belongs to the son himself!

(He attacks Gunther; clansmen try to separate them; Gunther dies from a sword thrust.)

Her den Ring!
                Now for the ring!

*(He reaches toward Siegfried's hand; it rises up menacingly. [3]
Gutrune screams in horror at Gunther's death. All are appalled and stand
stock-still. Brünnhilde appears from the river upstage, stepping
into the scene with grave decisiveness.)*

ACT 3

[1] A key moment Hagen has been working toward.

[2] And initiating another death struggle between brothers, like the one between Fasolt and Fafner in the Preamble.

[3] In other words, the ring pulls away from him—unlike earlier occasions where it let itself to be torn from its wearer's finger. But the ring is stolen goods—it belongs in the Rhine, it seems to control only Nibelungs, and Hagen has dwarf blood.

    Some audiences feel this is the dead Siegfried protecting the ring—but couldn't it be the ring protecting itself?

ACT 3

BRÜNNHILDE
(Still upstage)

Schweigt eures Jammers	Silence these waves
jauchzenden Schwall!	of screaming and wailing!
Das ihr Alle verrietet,	You all betrayed his wife,
zur Rache schreitet sein Weib.	and she's seeking retribution.

(She quietly comes farther downstage.)

Kinder hört' ich	I've heard children
greinen nach der Mutter,	crying to their mother
da süße Milch sie verschüttet:	over milk they'd spilled—
doch nicht erklang mir	but I've heard no sounds
würdige Klage,	of mourning suited
des höchsten Helden wert.	to the mightiest of heroes.

GUTRUNE
(Springing to her feet)

Brünnhilde! Neiderboste!	Brünnhilde! Envious woman!
Du brachtest uns diese Not:	You brought this evil on us—
die du die Männer ihm verhetztest,	you aroused the clansmen against him,
weh, daß du dem Haus genaht!	if only you hadn't come to this house!

BRÜNNHILDE

Armsel'ge, schweig!	Hush, you poor thing!
Sein Eheweib warst du nie:	You were never a proper wife—
als Buhlerin	only his mistress
bandest du ihn.	in a spurious marriage.
Sein Mannesgemahl bin ich,	I'm his lawful spouse,
der ewige Eide er schwur,	Siegfried and I swore eternal oaths
eh Siegfried je dich gesah.	before he ever laid eyes on you.

GUTRUNE
(Giving in to despair)

Verfluchter Hagen!	Curse you, Hagen!
Daß du das Gift mir rietest,	You counseled using the potion
das ihr den Gatten entrückt!	that stole her spouse away!
Ach, Jammer!	All this unhappiness!
Wie jäh nun weiß ich's:	At last I understand—
Brünnhild war die Traute,	Brünnhilde was his dearly beloved,
die durch den Trank er vergaß!	whom the drink made him forget!

(In shame she turns from Siegfried and bends in grief over Gunther's body [1]. She stays motionless in this position till the end. Meanwhile, at the other side of the stage and leaning defiantly on his spear and shield, Hagen is brooding somberly. [2] Alone at center stage, Brünnhilde contemplates Siegfried for some while, then turns gravely to the women and clansmen.)

ACT 3

Another postcard portrait.
1908 DRAWING OF BRÜNNHILDE
BY HEINRICH SCHLIMARSKI

[1] Textual note: p. 553 of the Dover full score (a facsimile of the 1877 Schott edition) inserts an odd qualifier here—*sich nun ersterbend*, "as if dying." Gutrune hasn't been physically injured, so this is puzzling enough that other editions omit it.

[2] Not surprising, because the ring unexpectedly pulled away from him.

ACT 3

BRÜNNHILDE
(To the clansmen)

Starke Scheite	Fetch a load
schichtet mir dort	of large lumber
am Rande des Rheins zu Hauf!	and raise a pyre on the riverbank!
Hoch und hell	Build a blaze
lodre die Glut,	that's high and bright,
die den edlen Leib	to consume the corpse
des hehresten Helden verzehrt.	of the world's noblest warrior.
Sein Roß führet daher,	Bring out his horse,
daß mit mir dem Recken es folge:	so we both can go with the hero—
denn des Helden heiligste	on this lofty occasion
Ehre zu teilen,	I long to share
verlangt mein eigner Leib.	personally in his triumph.
Vollbringt Brünnhildes Wort!	Perform these tasks for Brünnhilde!

(During the following, younger clansmen build a huge funeral pyre in front of the villa near the Rhine. Women cover it over, then sprinkle herbs and flowers on top. Brünnhilde sinks again into deep contemplation of the deceased Siegfried's face. She feels such tenderness, it transforms her features.)

Wie Sonne lauter	Like limpid sunshine
strahlt mir sein Licht:	his light streams over me—
der Reinste war er,	he was the purest of men,
der mich verriet!	yet he played me false!
Die Gattin trügend	He tricked his spouse
—treu dem Freunde—	while faithful to his friend;
von der eig'nen Trauten	from his own true love,
—einzig ihm teuer—	who stayed loyal to him,
schied er sich durch sein Schwert.	he separated himself with his sword.
Echter als Er	Nobody swore
schwur keiner Eide;	more solemn oaths;
treuer als Er	nobody entered into
hielt keiner Verträge;	more ethical agreements;
lautrer als Er	nobody ever loved
liebte kein Andrer!	more loyally than he!
Und doch, alle Eide,	And yet all his oaths,
alle Verträge,	all his agreements,
die treueste Liebe—	and the truest of all loves
trog keiner wie Er!	he betrayed like nobody before!
Wißt ihr wie das ward?	Can you say how this came about?

(Looking upward)

Oh, ihr, der Eide	Oh you, who've guarded
ewige Hüter!	oaths for all time!
Lenkt euren Blick	Turn your gaze
auf mein blühendes Leid;	on my overflowing grief;
erschaut eure ewige Schuld!	for all time, observe your guilt!

ACT 3

"See how gladly your wife greets you!"
1911 WATERCOLOR BY ARTHUR RACKHAM

ACT 3

Meine Klage hör,	Hear my accusation,
du hehrster Gott!	almighty god!
Durch seine tapferste Tat,	It was his very act of courage,
dir so tauglich erwünscht,	which you deeply desired,
weihtest du den,	that doomed him
der sie gewirkt,	when he did it
dem Fluche, dem du verfielest:	to the curse that claimed you—
mich mußte	I had to be
der Reinste verraten,	betrayed by that innocent soul
daß wissend würde ein Weib!	to become a woman of wisdom!
Weiß ich nun was dir frommt?	Now do I know what you need?
Alles, Alles,	It's all, all,
Alles weiß ich,	all too clear,
Alles ward mir nun frei!	now I completely understand!
Auch deine Raben	I hear your ravens
hör ich rauschen;	rustling nearby;
mit bang ersehnter Botschaft	I'll send the two of them home
send ich die beiden nun heim.	with tidings you fear yet hope for.
Ruhe, ruhe, du Gott!	Rest, O god! Go to your rest!

(She motions the clansmen to carry Siegfried's body to the pyre; meanwhile she takes the ring from his finger and examines it thoughtfully.)

Mein Erbe nun	My heritage
nehm ich zu eigen.	is in my hands.
Verfluchter Reif!	Damnable ring!
Furchtbarer Ring!	Dreaded band of gold!
Dein Gold faß ich,	I grasp you now
und geb es nun fort.	to give you away.
Der Wassertiefe	You wise sisters
weise Schwestern,	in the watery deep,
des Rheines schwimmende Töchter,	you gliding daughters of the Rhine,
euch dank ich redlichen Rat!	I'm grateful for your good advice!
Was ihr begehrt,	What you yearn for
ich geb es euch:	will soon be yours—
aus meiner Asche	pluck it from my ashes
nehmt es zu eigen!	and possess it again!
Das Feuer, das mich verbrennt,	The flames that will ravage me
rein'ge vom Fluche, den Ring!	will cleanse the curse from the ring!
Ihr in der Flut,	Deep in the waves
löset ihn auf,	it will dissolve,
und lauter bewahrt	then properly guard
das lichte Gold,	your pristine gold
das euch zum Unheil geraubt.	that was robbed with such evil results. [1]

(She puts on the ring and turns toward the pile of lumber over which Siegfried's body lies. She seizes an immense firebrand from a clansman and points upstage with it.)

[1] What "good advice" could the daughters have given her to cause this sea change? After all, she's known the truth since Day 1 when Wotan apprised her of the gold, the ring, the curse, his plans, the cost in lives, the full background. What's more, she's kept current: Siegfried himself updated her on later developments, likewise her sister Waltraute just two days back.

Even so, she repeatedly set those realities aside because she does her "thinking strictly with [her] heart," because the ring blessed her "with the light of Siegfried's love." Again, what could the daughters tell her that she hasn't known for decades?

One crucial fact: the reason for her husband's recent behavior. As the sprites told Siegfried himself, he's "a puppet and thoroughly blind . . . oblivious to his oaths . . . can't remember his runic lessons . . . was granted an incomparable gift which he's gotten rid of." And they know why: the dark elves drugged him, crippling his memory with a virulent form of selective amnesia.

Gutrune heard Brünnhilde laughing down by the river. Was it in relief at finding Siegfried was an "innocent soul" after all?

ACT 3

Fliegt heim, ihr Raben!	Fly home, ravens!
Raunt es eurem Herren,	Reveal to your lord
was hier am Rhein ihr gehört!	what you've learned by the Rhine!
An Brünnhildes Felsen	Pass Brünnhilde's mountain
fahrt vorbei!	as you make your way!
Der dort noch lodert,	Loge's still ablaze on top,
weiset Loge nach Walhall!	tell him Valhalla awaits him!
Denn der Götter Ende	The gods' passing is nigh,
dämmert nun auf.	twilight fades into night.
So werf ich den Brand	Thus the torch passes,
in Walhalls prangende Burg.	as will the proud castle of Valhalla.

(She hurls the firebrand into the pile of lumber, which instantly bursts into flame. Two ravens shoot above the rugged shoreline and vanish upstage. Brünnhilde catches sight of her horse, which two clansmen have just brought out.)

Grane, mein Roß!	Grane, my horse!
Sei mir gegrüßt!	Heartiest greetings!

(She runs up to him, instantly removes his bridle, leans close, and confides in him.)

Weißt du auch, mein Freund,	Can you tell, my friend,
wohin ich dich führe?	where I'm taking you?
Im Feuer leuchtend,	Your lord's lying there,
liegt dort dein Herr,	lit by the fire,
Siegfried, mein seliger Held.	Siegfried, my sacred hero.
Dem Freunde zu folgen,	Being near your friend
wieherst du freudig?	makes you neigh with joy?
Lockt dich zu ihm	Is the laughing fire
die lachende Lohe?	luring you to him?
Fühl meine Brust auch,	Feel how fiercely
wie sie entbrennt,	it burns in my bosom,
helles Feuer	brilliant flames
das Herz mir erfaßt,	clutching my heart,
ihn zu umschlingen,	urging me to hold him
umschlossen von ihm,	closely to me,
in mächtigster Minne	in deepest devotion
vermählt ihm zu sein!	wedded to him!
Heiajaho! Grane!	Heiajaho! Grane!
Grüß deinen Herren!	Greet your lord!
Siegfried! Siegfried! Sieh!	Siegfried! Siegfried! Look!

(She vaults onto the horse and rears back for a jump.)

Selig grüßt dich dein Weib!	See how gladly your wife greets you!

(She urges the horse onto the pyre in a single bound. At once the blaze flares up so that flames fill the whole area in front of the villa and seem about to overwhelm the villa itself. Terrified, clansmen and women rush downstage. The entire playing area appears to catch on fire, then the glow suddenly dies down, leaving a smoky, drifting haze upstage that congeals into a dark cloud on the horizon. Meanwhile the Rhine rises, overruns

ACT 3

Woglinde and Welgunde swim up and drag him into the depths.
1896 PAINTING BY FERDINAND LEEKE

ACT 3

its banks, and extinguishes the blaze. Riding the waves, the three Rhine daughters appear on the smoldering stage. After Brünnhilde took possession of the ring, Hagen has been watching her with growing anxiety, now he panics at the sight of the Rhine daughters. He hurls his helmet, shield, and spear aside and rushes madly into the flood tide.)

HAGEN

Zurück vom Ring!   Get away from the ring!

(Woglinde and Welgunde swim up, wrap their arms around his neck, and drag him into the depths. [1] Flosshilde in front, they all swim upstage, exultantly displaying their recovered ring. A reddish glow breaks through the dark cloud on the horizon, growing continually brighter. In its light we see the three Rhine daughters playing joyously with the ring in the heart of the Rhine, whose waters have receded and gradually returned to their bed. Standing among the remains of the devastated villa, women and clansmen watch, profoundly moved, as the fiery glow keeps growing in the sky. [2] When its brightness is finally at its peak, we see Valhalla's throne room with the gods and heroes sitting in conference just as Waltraute described them in Act 1. Brilliant flames arise and invade the gods' throne room. The flames completely engulf the gods as the curtain closes.) [3]

END OF THE RING CYCLE

ACT 3

[1] One last time we hear the motif of the curse on the ring:

It surges up in the orchestra, then is cut off halfway through.

[2] A reminder: per the 3rd Norn, Wotan himself ignites Valhalla and brings about the gods' passing—by plunging his "shattered spear . . . into Loge's fiery breast."

The status quo ante has been restored. The god can now obey Brünnhilde's injunction, "Go to your rest!"

[3] It's Brünnhilde who gets the last word, musically speaking. At the very end, the orchestra plays the exultant motif in Act 3 of *The Valkyrie* that Sieglinde sang when praising Brünnhilde:

The lines that go with the music are: "Oh greatest of marvels! You magnificent girl!"

So she is.

Valhalla going up in flames.
DESIGN FOR THE 1894 BAYREUTH
RING BY MAX BRUCKNER

ACT 3

LOOKING BACK ON
TWILIGHT FOR THE GODS

What ultimately happened?
    1) Because oaths and agreements still function, the dark elves exploit them.
    2) After extracting a confession from Siegfried, Hagen executes him.
    3) Hagen finally lays claim to the ring but is rebuffed and fails.
    4) The water sprites induce Brünnhilde to change her thinking.
    5) Brünnhilde immolates herself and relinquishes the ring.
    6) The Rhine River recovers its gold.
    7) The status quo ante has been restored—the gods can justly pass away and do.

What's left?
    1) Earth, air, fire, water, and the gold in its natural state.
    2) Trees, fish, songbirds, bears, wolves, foxes, deer, and other life-forms.
    3) Water sprites, Gibichungs, Neidings, other clanspeople, and dwarf workers.
    4) Fair dealing and truth telling as ideals.
    5) Alberich.

What isn't?
    1) Giants.
    2) The World Ash Tree and its well of wisdom.
    3) Gods, goddesses, zombie warriors, and Wälsungs.
    4) Hunding, Mime, Gunther, and Hagen.
    6) Valhalla and the house of Gibich.

Love's latest role?
    Self-sacrifice for the greater good.

1911 PEN DRAWING BY ARTHUR RACKHAM

TIMELINE OF THE ENTIRE RING CYCLE

Before the Cycle Begins

* In early manhood, Wotan visits the World Ash Tree and drinks from its well of wisdom.
    — He gives one of his eyes to pay for the privilege.
    — He breaks a limb from the tree and whittles it into a spear.
    — Using this as his scepter, he rules as protector of agreements and oaths.

* He marries Fricka, gaining a sister-in-law and two brothers-in-law.

* He encounters Loge as a fire spirit and presses him into the gods' service.

* Wotan's vanity and insecurity increase.
    — At the same time, the World Ash Tree deteriorates.

Preamble: *The Rhine Gold*

* Alberich meets the Rhine daughters and steals their gold.
    — He forges the gold into a magic ring.
    — He enslaves his fellow Nibelungs.

* Wotan, a good ruler going bad, hires Fasolt and Fafner to build him a royal castle.
    — They ask to be paid with Alberich's stolen gold.
    — Instead of returning the gold to the Rhine, Wotan agrees.
    — He and Loge capture Alberich in his underground realm.
    — They take Alberich's treasure, tarnhelmet, and ring.
    — Alberich puts a curse on the ring, promising misery and doom to wearers.

TIMELINE OF THE ENTIRE RING CYCLE

* Wotan hands the treasure to the giants but holds on to the ring.
    — The oracle Erda urges him to give it up.
    — He turns it over to the giants and fulfills his agreement.

* Fafner kills Fasolt and hides in a forest.
    — He changes into a dragon to guard the ring and treasure.

* The gods dwell in their new castle, now called Valhalla.
    — Wotan sees the ring is a danger and must be returned to the Rhine.
    — Going from bad to worse, he devises a scheme for getting around his agreement.

Day 1: *The Valkyrie*

* Wotan mates with a human woman.
    — She bears him fraternal twins, Siegmund and Sieglinde.
    — Wotan trains Siegmund and gives him a magic sword for killing Fafner.
    — The twins become lovers.

* Loge leaves the gods and changes back into a fire spirit.

* Wotan visits the oracle Erda to gain knowledge.
    — She bears him nine daughters: Brünnhilde and the Valkyries.
    — They raise an army of slain warriors to guard Valhalla.

* Fricka shows Wotan that his plan would destroy both his regime and his legacy.
    — Siegmund's seizure of the ring would demolish them as promptly as if Wotan seized it himself.
    — It would topple the two ethical pillars the god has erected: fair dealing and truth telling.
    — They at least can remain after him (and do) but not if he himself has undermined them.

* Wotan orders Siegmund's death, but Brünnhilde tries to save the twins.
    — The god intervenes and breaks Siegmund's sword; Siegmund dies.
    — Pregnant with Siegmund's son, Sieglinde flees with the broken sword.
    — Wotan punishes Brünnhilde, leaving her asleep behind a wall of fire.
    — He grounds the Valkyries and their zombie army.
    — Reaching his rock bottom, he recognizes his powerlessness.

Day 2: *Siegfried*

* Wotan goes on a pilgrimage for nearly a generation.
    — Dressed as a wanderer, he seeks further wisdom.

* Meanwhile, the pregnant Sieglinde collapses in a forest close to the dragon's lair.
    — She's rescued by the dwarf Mime and dies giving birth to Siegfried.
    — Mime raises the boy to slay the dragon and capture the ring.

* Wotan returns but avoids Siegfried, so the boy remains independent.
    — Instead, he offers aid to Mime and Alberich, with no immediate result.

TIMELINE OF THE ENTIRE RING CYCLE

* Siegfried reforges the broken sword.
    — Mime manipulates him into slaying Fafner.
    — The boy takes the ring and tarnhelmet without breaking Wotan's agreement.
    — Mime tries to kill him but dies when Siegfried strikes first.
    — A Woodbird guides Siegfried to a girl who can be his companion.

* Wotan blocks the boy's way, deliberately provoking a showdown.
    — Siegfried smashes his scepter and ends the god's rule.

* Siegfried finds the sleeping Brünnhilde, wakes her, and weds her.

Day 3: *Twilight for the Gods*

* Wotan surrounds Valhalla with a pyre, which he'll one day set ablaze.
    — He and the castle's residents wait for the ring's return to the Rhine.
    — The god's legacy, his ideals of fair dealing and truth telling, will live on.

* Meanwhile Brünnhilde tutors Siegfried as they happily cohabit.
    — Ultimately, he goes out exploring, leaving the ring with her.

* The Gibichungs, human relatives of Alberich, trick and drug Siegfried.
    — Siegfried kidnaps Brünnhilde for them and reclaims the ring.
    — Furious, Brünnhilde conspires with them to execute Siegfried.
    — They succeed but don't recover the ring.

* Brünnhilde repents after the Rhine daughters visit her.
    — She burns Siegfried's body, returns the ring to the river, and dies herself.
    — Wotan torches Valhalla; the gods pass away as survivors watch.

1910 PEN DRAWING BY ARTHUR RACKHAM.

WHAT THE CYCLE DOES . . . AND DOESN'T

The Nibelung's Ring Shows Us
1) A wrongdoer whose crime threatens the whole community.
2) A peacekeeper who doesn't rectify the crime or remove the threat.
3) His later efforts to accomplish both through third parties.
4) The prolonged harm this causes innocent individuals.
5) The peacekeeper's failure due to fears and muddled thinking.
6) His education and growth through loss and suffering.
7) The wisdom of surrendering control and trusting the universe.
8) The roles of compassion, acceptance, and sacrifice in rectifying a crime.
9) The helpful contributions even wrongdoers can make.
10) The countless combinations and permutations the process requires.
11) And the time it takes.

It Particularly Shows Older Generations Abusing the Younger
1) Its elders generate conflicts and difficulties, then look to their descendants to resolve them.
2) The Cycle gives several instances: Wotan and Siegmund, Mime and Siegfried, Alberich and Hagen.
3) Through selfishness and micromanagement, the elders cause immense suffering.
4) It takes the education and self-sacrifice of a loving daughter to finally restore peace.
5) The Cycle's composer also addresses this issue in *The Master Singers of Nuremberg* and *Parsifal*.
6) "The sins of the father are to be laid upon the children."—Shakespeare, *The Merchant of Venice*.

Yet It Also Shows an Elder Stepping Down for the Public Good
1) Unhinged by the collapse of his plans, Wotan commits many damaging actions.
2) He slays Hunding and Siegmund, punishes Brünnhilde, then abandons his Valkyries and warriors.
3) Afterward, he goes on a generation-long pilgrimage, then returns changed and accepting.
4) He understands that his regime has failed and the gods must go.
5) He aids the dark elves because they, too, can contribute to the peace process.
6) After rigorously avoiding Siegfried, he deliberately provokes the boy to end his rule.
7) His regime over, he reduces the World Ash Tree to a pyre around Valhalla.
8) He gathers his colleagues, waits scrupulously in his throne room, and doesn't intervene in events.
9) His ravens report doings below, and he only torches Valhalla after peace has been restored.
10) His legacy lives on, though others besides Hagen may misuse his ideals in ages to come.
11) In *The Master Singers of Nuremberg*, the Cycle's composer also has an elder step down for the public good.

WHAT THE CYCLE DOES... AND DOESN'T

Four Things the Cycle *Doesn't* Show Us

1) Who the Rhine Daughters' Father Is

The Cycle never names him. Some audiences feel he's Father Rhine (German *Vater Rhein*, Latin *Rhenus Pater*), the Rhine's personification, its river god, a figure comparable to Neptune in Celtic and German legends. The Roman poet Martial called him the "father of water nymphs and watercourses." His powers could be greater than Wotan's: he's a force of nature.

2) Why the Sprites Make Trouble for Themselves

The Rhine daughters take center stage twice, and on both occasions, they blurt out remarks that cause enormous trouble for themselves and the community. In *The Rhine Gold*, they mortify Alberich, then chatter about the gold's magical potential. If they'd kept still, there would be no theft—and no Cycle.

Generations later, in *Twilight for the Gods*, they do much the same with Siegfried: he's ready to give them the ring, but when they lecture him on its perils, he changes his mind and keeps it. Had they stayed silent, four more cast members would survive, and the audience could go home.

In both encounters, then, the sprites manufacture trouble for themselves. Why take such a risk? Do the daughters feel that warnings of sacrifice and disaster will discourage would-be thieves, that they're a deterrent that has succeeded in the past? The Cycle doesn't explain the girls' intentions. But we do have the Wanderer's maxim to explain the results: "Everything remains true to itself." In this case, both Alberich and Siegfried are rare individuals—the dwarf easily gives up love, and the human is insensitive to fear. So the daughters' warnings backfire.

3) What Causes Alberich to Behave as He Does

We aren't clear on why Alberich does evil. We understand the Cycle's other malefactors: Hagen schemes out of filial obedience; Mime has the vindictiveness of the bullied and downtrodden; Wotan's pride and fears lead to his white-collar villainies in the Preamble. But Alberich's motivations aren't so definite.

Here's how he behaves: he molests the Rhine daughters, steals their gold, persecutes his own kind, seeks world domination, wants to destroy the gods, and lives only to recover the ring. Some audiences feel he does so because the sprites reject him, because he's unlucky in love. The dwarf himself offers that excuse, later claiming he "reacted to his need, disgrace, and fit of fury." But in fact, his theft shows calculation and premeditation: he sounds out the sprites on the gold, coolly weighs its advantages ("The earth's riches are mine if I mold that substance?"), then steals it with all the speed he can summon.

Consequently, his rejection by the sprites doesn't seem adequate motivation for all the harm he causes. And another dishonesty may lurk behind this excuse: there are female dwarves. Why would Alberich look for affection elsewhere? Maybe such dishonesties underlie his calling others thieves but not himself.

What motivations might be more believable? Here's a piece of speculation based on the Cycle's linking Alberich and the fugitive Siegmund: at the latter's entrance, the orchestra echoes the music at Alberich's arrival onstage, trussed up and in Wotan's power. The implication is that both are under the god's control, but could the two be similar in other ways? Siegmund's a lonely outcast at odds with humanity. Might Alberich be in similar straits with his fellow Nibelungs? If yes, then it would supply a stronger motive for his wooing far afield, his fascism, his persecution of his own people. But the Cycle never says so. By saying nothing, is the Cycle admitting that evil still defies explanation?

4) Where the Peacemaking Power Comes From

What *force* or *source* finally restores peace and brings about the Cycle's serene conclusion? We only know what it isn't. It's not Erda's wisdom; she's gone into permanent hibernation. It's not fate or destiny; the Norns have snapped their thread and joined Erda. It's not nature; the sprites make mistakes, and the Woodbird runs from Wotan's ravens. And it's not the race of gods; they've stepped down and can only wait for the end.

Nor is it the band of gold itself; unlike Tolkien's ring, it has remained largely passive, returning to the river through the actions of others. How about Father Rhine? The spirit of justice? Christianity? Evolution? Bernard Shaw's "life force"? The Cycle doesn't finger any of these suspects. Could some philosophical or psychological concept be at work? We've noted Brünnhilde's gift of "thinking with her heart" and the Wanderer's maxim that "everything remains true to itself." Are these candidates? It's unlikely: each is mentioned only once in the libretto; neither can qualify as the *Ring*'s mantra.

Admittedly, the composer's final opera *does* offer an altruistic concept as an answer to human woes. In *Parsifal*, the chain of suffering is snapped by a benign characteristic, the virtue of *mitleid* (compassion or empathy). Yes, Brünnhilde and Siegmund display this trait, but the Cycle never identifies it as such. Moreover, *Parsifal* offers it as the insight of a single individual, while in *The Nibelung's Ring*, attaining peace is clearly a *group process*.

That process has been long, involved, and the outcome of "countless combinations and permutations." Look at what the ring undergoes in order to return home: (1) Wotan takes it from the thief; (2) he gives it to Fafner; (3) the twins breed a rescuer; (4) dwarves coerce him to kill Fafner; (5) natural forces advise him to get the ring; (6) the rescuer gives it to his wife; (7) dwarves coerce him to take it back; (8) dwarves kill the rescuer; (9) natural forces advise his wife to reclaim the ring; (10) she finally returns it to its home. And that's just a bare-bones outline.

Plus, there's a subsidiary question that isn't answered. Three cast members correctly *prophesy* the Cycle's outcome, in whole or in part: Sieglinde, Brünnhilde, and Wotan. The Cycle doesn't give reasons for their accuracy, and Wotan's conviction is especially remarkable; he gives up his power and control yet seems certain of the result. How is this possible? A clue may lie in these two lines where he dismisses relying on destiny, fate, or the Norns:

> Im Zwange der Welt The world controls
> weben die Nornen   how they weave that thread

He's saying that the "world controls"—not him, not the usual suspects cited previously. What does this mean? Are we to trust in the world's workings? Is the "world itself" the greater force or source that can resolve problems to its general benefit? Once again, the Cycle doesn't say. Maybe good defies explanation, too.

1911 PEN DRAWING BY ARTHUR RACKHAM.

Related Resources

Barenboim, Daniel. Chorus and Orchestra of the Bayreuth Festival 1991–92. *Der Ring des Nibelungen*. Hamburg: Teldec 256467714, 1994, 14 CDs. Dynamic, reasonably priced performance in potent stereo; recommended despite the erratic synopses.

Bolen, Jean Shinoda. *Ring of Power: The Abandoned Child, the Authoritarian Father, and the Disempowered Feminine: A Jungian Understanding of Wagner's Ring Cycle*. San Francisco: Harper, 1992. The work as a case study of a dysfunctional family; by a clinical psychiatrist and often startlingly persuasive.

Cooke, Deryck. *An Introduction to* Der Ring des Nibelungen. With Georg Solti and the Vienna Philharmonic. London: Decca, 2005. Tried-and-true presentation of Wagner's leitmotifs; includes two CDs and a booklet.

DiGaetani, John Louis. *Richard Wagner: New Light on a Musical Life*. Jefferson, NC: McFarland, 2014. Blames Wagner's heirs for his abuse by Nazis; ramshackle writing, but the point needs making often.

Donington, Robert. *Wagner's "Ring" and Its Symbols*. 1st American ed. New York: St. Martins, 1974. Groundbreaking study of the Cycle as a gallery of Jungian archetypes.

Ewans, Michael. *Wagner and Aeschylus: The* Ring *and the* Oresteia. London: Faber, 1982. Investigates how the Cycle both emulates and refutes its ancient Greek predecessor.

Gollancz, Victor. *The Ring at Bayreuth: And Some Thoughts on Operatic Production*. New York: Dutton, 1966. Critique of Wieland Wagner's primitivist stagings at the 1965 festival.

Guhl-Miller, Solomon R. "The Path of Wagner's Wotan." PhD diss., Rutgers University, 2012. https://rucore.libraries.rutgers.edu/rutgers-lib/36610/PDF/1/play/. Traces the god's evolution into selflessness and acceptance of necessary change.

Hanslick, Eduard. "Richard Wagner's Stage Festival at Bayreuth (1876)." In *Music Criticisms*. Translated and edited by Henry Pleasants. Rev. ed. Harmonsworth, UK: Penguin, 1963. Detailed negative review of the Cycle's premiere; historically valuable.

Lee, M. Owen. Wagner: *The Terrible Man and His Truthful Art*. Toronto: University of Toronto Press, 1999. Eloquent exploration of Wagner's flawed, paradoxical genius.

Magee, Bryan. *Aspects of Wagner*. Rev. and enlarged ed. Oxford: Oxford University Press, 1988. Amazingly cogent essays on Wagner's dramaturgy, global influence, and criticism of Jewish culture.

Magee, Elizabeth, ed. *Legends of the Ring*. London: Folio Society, 2004. Handy anthology drawn from the verse and prose *Edda*s, *Volsunga Saga*, *Nibelungenlied*, and other early sources.

RELATED RESOURCES

———. *Richard Wagner and the Nibelungs*. Oxford: Oxford University Press, 1990. Catalogs Wagner's reading of Nordic literature and speculates on its contribution; compelling sidelights on Wotan.

Millington, Barry. *Wagner*. Rev. ed. Princeton, NJ: Princeton University Press, 1992. Compact study of Wagner's life, works, and values; stronger on musical than dramatic analysis.

Newman, Ernest. *The Life of Richard Wagner*. Vol. 2, *1848–1860*. New York: Knopf, 1937. Classic critical biography of Wagner's life and artistic evolution; some arbitrary judgments.

Osborne, Charles. *The Complete Operas of Richard Wagner*. North Pomfret, VT: Trafalgar, 1990. Capsule descriptions of the Cycle's sources and development; plot summaries are sometimes imprecise.

Porges, Heinrich. *Wagner Rehearsing the "Ring": An Eyewitness Account of the Stage Rehearsals of the First Bayreuth Festival*. Translated by Robert L. Jacobs. Cambridge, UK: Cambridge University Press, 1983. Records Wagner's last-minute revisions plus his instructions for interpretation, blocking, and business.

Ryde, P. J. "*Götterdämmerung*: Possible Solutions to Some Wagner Problems." In *Penetrating Wagner's Ring: An Anthology*, edited by John Louis DiGaetani. Cranbury, NJ: Associated University Presses, 1978. Addresses common misunderstandings concerning the gods' demise at the end of the Cycle.

Scruton, Roger. *The Ring of Truth: The Wisdom of Wagner's* Ring of the Nibelung. New York: Overlook, 2017. Lushly written musings that see empathy, sacrifice, and individual responsibility as the work's final messages.

Shaw, George Bernard. *The Perfect Wagnerite*. Chicago: Stone, 1899. Witty commentary that views the *Ring* as a parable of Victorian capitalism.

Spencer, Stewart. "Language and Sources of 'The Ring.'" In *The Rhinegold (Das Rheingold): Opera Guide 35*. London: Calder, 1985. Describes the libretto's borrowings, alliterative effects, and plot innovations.

Spencer, Stewart, Barry Millington, Elizabeth Magee, Roger Hollinrake, and Warren Darcy. *Wagner's* Ring of the Nibelung*: A Companion*. New York: Thames & Hudson, 1993. Scrupulous modern translation with extensive textual notes, plus commentaries by colleagues.

Stein, Jack M. *Richard Wagner and the Synthesis of the Arts*. Detroit: Wayne State University Press, 1960. Sees discrepancies between theory and practice in Wagner's mature style; some debatable conclusions.

Tanner, Michael. "An Introduction to the End." In *Twilight of the Gods (Götterdämmerung): Opera Guide 31*. London: Calder, 1985. Finds the Cycle's ending problematic; some misperceptions and misreadings.

Thielemann, Christian. *My Life with Wagner: Fairies, Rings, and Redemption: Exploring Opera's Most Enigmatic Composer*. New York: Pegasus, 2016. Learning, pondering, preparing, and conducting Wagner; an insider's look by a leading interpreter.

Turing, Penelope. *New Bayreuth*. 1969. Second impression. London: Neville Spearman, 1971. Chronicles Wieland Wagner's innovative productions and the less-influential ones of his brother Wolfgang.

RELATED RESOURCES

Wagner, Richard. *Götterdämmerung: In Full Score.* New York: Dover, 1982. A facsimile of the 1877 Schott edition, with front matter newly translated into English.

———. *The Nibelungen Myth.* Translated by William Ashton Ellis. In *Richard Wagner's Prose Works*, vol. 7 (London and Dresden). London: Kegan Paul, Trench, Trübner, 1898. http://users.belgacom.net/wagner library/prose/wagnibe.htm. The Cycle's initial scenario, drafted by Wagner in 1848.

———. *Das Rheingold: In Full Score.* New York: Dover, 1985. A facsimile of the 1873 Schott edition, with front matter newly translated into English.

———. *Siegfried: In Full Score.* New York: Dover, 1983. A facsimile of the 1876 Schott edition, with front matter newly translated into English.

———. *Die Walküre: In Full Score.* New York: Dover, 1978. A facsimile of the C. F. Peters edition, published ca. 1910, with front matter newly translated into English.

Walter, Frederick Paul. "Wagner and the Generation Gap: Program Note for *Die Meistersinger*." Chicago: Lyric Opera, November 1977. Explores Wagner's earlier treatment of oppression by elders—and how the old can give way to the new.

White, David. *The Turning Wheel: A Study of Contracts and Oaths in Wagner's* Ring. Cranbury, NJ: Associated University Presses, 1988. Argues that Wotan's ideals of fair dealing and truth telling weren't ideal after all.

1910 PEN DRAWING BY ARTHUR RACKHAM

About the Contributors

RICHARD WAGNER

Renaissance man and all-purpose theater professional, Richard Wagner not only supplied the music but also penned his own librettos, while functioning as conductor, stage director, impresario, and fundraiser. Born in Leipzig in 1813, he completed thirteen operas, though the first three are rarely staged. His later works range from modern folklore (*The Flying Dutchman*) to historical Germany (*Tannhäuser, Lohengrin, The Master Singers of Nuremberg*) to myth and legend (*The Nibelung's Ring, Tristan and Isolde, Parsifal*). These galvanized Europe's lyric theater, the drama coming first and supported by the music, in contrast to the arbitrary stage action and shoehorned arias typical of the time. The political upheavals of 1848 turned Wagner into a man without a country, hounded by creditors and in continual turmoil until taken late in life under the wing of Bavaria's King Ludwig II. He then built his own playhouse in Bayreuth, launching several innovations (continental seating, darkened house lights, sunken pit) that are commonplace in live theater today. He died in Venice in 1883.

FREDERICK PAUL WALTER

A scriptwriter, fine arts broadcaster, publicist, translator, and college theater director, Frederick Paul Walter has worked for Lyric Opera of Chicago, Houston Grand Opera, Opera Southwest, and other performance organizations, likewise for NPR stations KUHF in Houston and KQED in San Francisco. He also serves as moderator of HomageToArthurRubinstein@groups.io, a celebration of one of history's greatest concert pianists. Walter has written about classical music and opera for nearly half a century, in particular penning reviews, program notes, and on-air presentations of Wagner's *Ring* and *Master Singers of Nuremberg*. Donning a different hat, Walter has also published modern translations of eight science fiction thrillers by French novelist Jules Verne for State University of New York, University of Nebraska, and Wesleyan University. He now lives in Albuquerque, New Mexico.

www.ingramcontent.com/pod-product-compliance
Lightning Source LLC
Chambersburg PA
CBHW060419300426
44111CB00018B/2911